A Short History of EGYPT

Other publications by the same author

Britain and the Arab States, Luzac, 1948.
Ptolemaic Temples, Waterloo Printing Co., 1977.
Le Trésor de Toutankhamon, Hasso Ebeling, 1980.
Les Trésors de Babylone, Hasso Ebeling, 1981.
Blue Guide to Egypt, with Peter Stocks, Benn, 1983, 2nd ed. A. & C. Black,
    1988.
El Amarna, Waterloo Printing Co., 1984.
Egyptian Poems, Merlin Books, 1987.
Egyptian Legends and Stories, The Rubicon Press Ltd., 1988.
The Road to el-Aguzein (autobiography), Kegan Paul International, 1988.

A Short History of EGYPT

M.V. SETON-WILLIAMS

The Rubicon Press

In memory of Professor Sir Ernest Scott

The Rubicon Press Limited
57 Cornwall Gardens
London SW7 4BE

British Library Cataloguing in Publication Data

Seton-Williams, M.V.
    A short history of Egypt.
    I. Title
    962

ISBN 0-948695-12-9

Designed and typeset by The Rubicon Press
Printed and bound in Great Britain by Biddles Limited of Guildford and
   King's Lynn

CONTENTS

LIST OF ILLUSTRATIONS

FOREWORD

Very few of the people who visit Egypt each year have any idea of its history. This book is an endeavour to fill that gap and is intended as an introduction to the country.

Naturally it is very abbreviated as one cannot deal with five thousand years of history in detail, but the author is supremely well qualified to do so, if anyone can. Dr. Seton-Williams trained with Sir Flinders Petrie and her knowledge of early Egypt is encyclopaedic. She also has a deep love of the Egyptian people and the book is infused with her sympathy and understanding of them. One could not have a better introduction to the subject than she provides.

The late Sir Colin Crowe
British Chargé d'Affaires
Egypt
(1959-1961)

HISTORICAL SUMMARY

Prehistoric Period		prior to	c. 3400 B.C.
Predynastic Period			c. 3400 - 3100 B.C.
Archaic Period	(Dynasty I		c. 3100 - 2890 B.C.
	(Dynasty II		c. 2890 - 2886 B.C.
Old Kingdom	(Dynasty III		c. 2886 - 2613 B.C.
	(Dynasty IV		c. 2613 - 2494 B.C.
	(Dynasty V		c. 2494 - 2345 B.C.
	(Dynasty VI		c. 2345 - 2181 B.C.
First Intermediate Period	(Dynasty VII		c. 2181 - 2173 B.C.
	(Dynasty VIII		c. 2173 - 2160 B.C.
	(Dynasty IX		c. 2160 - 2130 B.C.
	(Dynasty X		c. 2130 - 2040 B.C.
Middle Kingdom	(Dynasty XI		c. 2133 - 1991 B.C.
	(Dynasty XII		c. 1991 - 1786 B.C.
Second Intermediate Period	(Dynasties XIII-XVI		c. 1796 - 1567 B.C.) partly
	(Dynasty XVII		c. 1650 - 1567 B.C.) overlapping
New Kingdom	(Dynasty XVIII		c. 1567 - 1320 B.C.
	(Dynasty XIX		c. 1320 - 1200 B.C.
	(Dynasty XX		c. 1200 - 1085 B.C.
Third Intermediate Period	(Dynasty XXI		c. 1085 - 945 B.C.
	(Dynasty XXII		945 - 715 B.C.) partly
	(Dynasty XXIII		818 - 715 B.C.) overlapping
	(Dynasty XXIV		727 - 715 B.C.
	(Dynasty XXV (Kushite)		747 - 656 B.C.
	(*Assyrians in Egypt,*		
	(*sack of Memphis by*		
	(*Esahaddon*		671 B.C.
	(*Sack of Thebes by*		
	(*Assurbanipal*		663 B.C.
	(Dynasty XXVI (Saite)		664 - 525 B.C.
	(*Persian invasion*		525 B.C.
	(Dynasty XXVII) Under		525 - 404 B.C.
	(Dynasty XXIX) Persian		399 - 380 B.C.
	( ) Empire		
	(Dynasty XXX		380 - 343 B.C.
	(*Return of the Persians*		343 B.C.
	(Dynasty XXXI (Persians)		343 - 332 B.C.
	Alexander the Great		332 - 323 B.C.

Ptolemaic Period	332 - 30 B.C.
Roman Empire	30 B.C. - A.D. 363
Byzantine Empire	A.D. 363 - 642
Persian Invasions under Chosroes	A.D. 616 - 626/7
Flight of Muhammed to Medina.	
Beginning of Muslim Calendar	
Anno Hagera = A.H.	A.D. 622
Death of Prophet Muhammed	A.D. 632
Muslim Invasion of Egypt	A.D. 640 - 641
Orthodox Khalifs	A.D. 632 - 661
Umayyad Khalifs at Damascus	A.D. 661 - 750
Abbasid Khalifs at Baghdad and Samarra	A.D. 750 - 1258
Egypt governed by Governors serving	
Khalifs until A.D. 934 often semi-	
independent	
Tulunids (I) (I = Independent rulers)	A.D. 868 - 905
Ikshids (I)	A.D. 934 - 969
Fatamids claiming to be Khalifs (Shi'as)	A.D. 969 - 1171
Ayyubites recognizing Abbasid Khalifs	
(Sunnis)	A.D. 1171 - 1252
Mamluks	A.D. 1252 - 1517
Bahrite Mamluks (Turcoman)	A.D. 1252 - 1382
Circassian Mamluks	A.D. 1382 - 1517
Monol invasion of Iraq and Persia.	
Destruction of Baghdad	A.D. 1258
Puppet Khalifs brought to Cairo	A.D. 1258 - 1517
Ottoman Empire - Egypt governed	
through Turkish Pashas	A.D. 1517 - 1922
French invasion under Bonaparte	A.D. 1798
Muhammad Ali	A.D. 1805 - 1848
Khedives	A.D. 1805 - 1922
Fuad and Farouk, Kings	A.D. 1922 - 1952
Presidents of the Egyptian Republic:	
General Muhammad Neguib	June 1953 - Nov. 1954
	(Deposed)
Colonel Gamal Abdel Nasser	Nov. 1954 - Sept. 1970
	(Died)
Colonel Muhammad Anwar Sadat	Sept. 1970 - Oct. 1981
	(Assassinated)
Lt. General Muhammad Hosni Mubarak	Oct. 1981 -

PREFACE

Good history combines the great outline and the significant detail.

Sir Lewis Narmer

In 1917, I put down what I considered to be a most inadequate history of Egypt and decided to embark on one of my own. Here, seventy years later, are the fruits of that decision. Originally I had intended writing a long history, but was dissuaded by a fellow Australian who suggested that what was needed was a succinct account for the traveller to Egypt, which would embody the history up to the present day with some details of the everyday life and religion of the country.

This book can only serve as an introduction to Egypt - a land that has the longest continuous civilization in the world. If it spurs its reader to more serious study, it will have served its purpose.

ACKNOWLEDGEMENTS

I would like to thank the Tate Gallery, London for permission to reproduce the picture of Muhammad Ali by Sir David Wilkie; the Trustees of the British Museum for the King List; T.G.H. James for the list of Egyptian kings from his *Introduction to Ancient Egypt*; Ann Pemberton for the photographs of a street market in Aswan, the water-wheel at Saqqara and the carpet weavers near Giza; Leo Perk Vlanderaan for the photograph of Osiris, Anubis and Horus the Elder; Angela Godfrey for the photographs of the temple of Hatshepsut at Deir el-Bahari, the mosque of Abu el-Haggag at Luxor and a pilgrim's house on the West Bank, Thebes, also for typing and editing my manuscript. I would also like to thank Anthea Page and Juanita Homan of the Rubicon Press for all their help.

LAND AND RESOURCES

No country has had the long unbroken history that Egypt had in ancient times. For over 3,000 years, until taken by the Romans and added to their empire in 30 B.C., Egypt had been one of the most advanced and civilized countries of the world. Occupying a unique position in the north-east corner of Africa, it is the gateway to the Middle East and to India, and fronts onto the Mediterranean and Europe. Protected by the sea to the north and east, and fringed by deserts to the west and south, there was no immediate threat to its frontiers by powerful nations, and it was able to develop in its own way, at its own pace. Secure behind her deserts, this narrow land stretching for hundreds of miles, but scarcely ever wider than five or six miles on each side of the Nile, was curiously self-sufficient. Able to supply nearly all their basic needs, with the exception of timber and some minerals, the Egyptians considered themselves as the one 'true people', rather like the ancient Chinese did, and regarded the rest of the world as barbarians.

The name Egypt, now called by its ancient name Misr, comes from the Greek term *Aigyptos*, which in turn probably derived from *ḥwt-k3-Ptḥ* (Hikuptah), one of the many old names of Memphis, the capital of Egypt up to the end of the Old Kingdom. The division between Upper and Lower Egypt has never been very precisely determined; it is usually taken to be in the region of modern Cairo, whereas in ancient times Memphis was regarded as the 'Balance of the Two Lands'. Upper Egypt was known in Pharaonic times as Shemau and was divided into twenty-two administrative districts, known from their Greek name as nomes, starting in the south with Elephantine. Lower Egypt was known as To-Mehu and like Upper Egypt was also divided into nomes, the number of which varied from time to time, but were usually about twenty. The first nome in Lower Egypt was regarded as that of Memphis. Upper and Lower Egypt have always presented different problems

1

and the union of the Two Lands was a recurring theme in Egyptian history. Even today, there are marked regional differences with local dialects and different attitudes.

The ancient Egyptians called the Nile Valley Kemet, the 'Black Land', which referred to the dark silt brought down by the Nile. The desert was described as Deshet or the 'Red Land'. Egypt is clearly divided into two parts - the Two Lands of the records - the fan-shaped Delta, flat and once largely covered by papyrus swamps where birds lived and cattle roamed, and the river valley of Upper Egypt narrowly encompassed between the Libyan Hills to the west and the Eastern Desert and the Red Sea Hills to the east. The Nile, after finally breaking through the granite barrier of the First Cataract at Aswan, ancient Elephantine, passes north towards the sea, first through sandstone, then limestone beds that form the cliffs on either side of the river valley and which provided excellent building stone for the numerous tombs and temples built by the Egyptians. At one time, the Nile had as many as seven branches flowing through the Delta, now only the Rosetta and Damietta branches remain. The total area of Egypt is about 386,872 square miles (1,002,000 sq. km.) but the cultivated and settled area is only about 13,737 square miles (35,580 sq. km.), with the Nile, lakes and marshes occupying 2,800 square miles (7,252 sq. km.).

The Nile is the longest river in Africa. Without it, life in Egypt would be impossible. Its most important feature, beyond the presence of its water, was the annual inundation caused by rains which fell in Central Africa and in the Ethiopian Highlands. By the end of May, the river was usually at its lowest level. In June, in the area of Egypt proper, that is between Aswan and Cairo, the river would begin to rise. During August it normally rose even more and assumed a rich red colour, caused by the mud brought down from the Atbara and the Blue Nile. The water slowly spread out, remaining for several weeks, and during this period the mud carried in the flood water was deposited in a thin layer over the land. Recently, the flow of the Nile has been controlled and instead of an annual inundation there has been a change to perennial irrigation. The change began in the last century with the construction of a series of barrages at Esna, Nag Hammadi and Asyut, the last one being built before the Second World War. In the 1960s,

2

the Sudd el-Ali, or High Dam, was constructed, damming the river above Aswan and making a reservoir, known as Lake Nasser, some 500 kilometres long, up to and including Wadi Halfa in the Sudan. Up until recently, the rise of the Nile from ancient times to the present day seems to have reached much the same level. However, over the last eight years the rains and snows have not fallen in Equatorial Africa and the Ethiopian Highlands, so that the annual rise in the Nile has not taken place. This must also have happened in antiquity, as we have records of poor Niles in the First Intermediate Period. The Famine Stela, found on Sehail Island, purports to record a series of low Niles at the time of Djoser of the Third Dynasty (c. 2660 B.C.) and again at the end of the Twentieth Dynasty. There are no records of the exact length of time that these low Niles lasted but conditions nowadays, with the larger population, more extensive agricultre and industrial demands does not conform to the problems of earlier periods. The recent dry cycle was broken by heavy rains in the Sudan in 1988.

Village during the Inundation

BOATS - In ancient times the river was the main highway, both for goods and for people. Nowadays, more use is made of the roads which were not passable during the annual inundation and basin irrigation. Today most of the heavy river traffic is in Lower and Middle Egypt on large sailing boats called *markabs*. These mainly carry grain, stone for building and pottery. Barges carry fuel and sugar-cane, besides general cargo. Small sailing boats with lateen sails, called *feluccas*, carry passengers and act as ferries. Up until the advent of paddle steamers, large sailing vessels called *dahab-iyahs* could be chartered to carry tourists in the nineteenth century. Transport on the Nile was made easy by the prevailing wind from the north. This meant that vessels were able to sail upstream against the current and be rowed or drift downstream with it. During the annual inundation, flat-bottomed barges were used to transport building-stone and large statues straight from the quarries in the cliffs, adjacent to the river at Aswan and Silsileh, to where they would be used in the temples or tombs being built just beyond the outer limit of the flood waters.

RAW MATERIALS - Normally Egypt was confined to the extent of the Nile valley. However, during the period of the New Kingdom, the so-called Egyptian Empire controlled an area that extended as far south as the Fourth Cataract beyond Meroe and Kaima in Nubia. There, the Egyptians established a series of forts that also acted as trading posts with the local tribesmen, and obtained in exchange for Egyptian manufactured goods, wood for bows, gold, ivory, slaves and mercenaries. Diorite, gold and copper came from the Nubian desert and the Red Sea hills, quartzite, alabaster and many semi-precious stones came from the surrounding deserts. Turquoise, lapis lazuli and copper ores came from Sinai. Later, iron ore was found in the Aswan area and the Bahriyah Oasis. Natrun, used for purification and embalming, came from the Wadi Natrun, north-west of Cairo. The Eastern Desert was exploited for its gold and porphyry. It was a harsh land without proper water supplies and the quarrying was done mainly by prisoners. Nubia and Sinai were first explored by military expeditions and then their minerals and stone were exploited by gangs sent by the Egyptian government under military command. Mining ceased

Felucca loaded with chaff

when labour became too expensive but the possibilities of doing so are now being re-examined. Oil was first discovered in Egypt in 1909 A.D. but for a long time production was low. It is now sufficient to meet the country's requirements and the surplus is exported. At the moment, the Red Sea and Sinai are being surveyed for more fields. Natural gas has been found in the Delta and there are other fields in the Western Desert. Other minerals discovered include manganese and uranium.

THE OASES - In addition to the Nile valley, there is cultivation in the oases. The closest and the most important is the Faiyum, watered by a branch of the Nile called the Bahr Yussef. This has always been a rich garden area and contains a lake, the Birket Qarun, which is noted for its bird life. There are several other oases lying to the west of the Nile, the most southerly being el-Khargah, which is joined to the smaller oasis of el-Dakhlah. The northern oasis of el-Bahriyah is close to the Giza province, and is joined to el-Farafrah further to the south, which used to be administered from the seventh Upper Egyptian nome. The oases were linked with the Nile valley by a series of desert tracks and were used as a place of banishment for political prisoners. The Egyptians feared the desert and disliked the 'sand dwellers', the Bedouin tribes, that lived there. The desert was for them the haunt of giant serpents, evil spirits and symbolized privation, as their life was centred on the rich green Nile valley. They only left the valley with reluctance and returned to it as speedily as possible. The word for foreign country was written in hieroglyphs as 'three hills', which was what the Egyptians could see on their horizon as they looked out on the deserts.

AGRICULTURE - In historic times, the economy of Egypt was based on agriculture. During normal years when the inundation was sufficient, which is to say, a flood of between six to seven metres deep, the Egyptian peasant (*fellahin*) got a good return from the land - much better than other countries in the Middle East - because of the rich silt in which the crops were grown. The country's tax system was based on the Nile, so that if the inundation was poor, taxes were reduced. Until recently, Egypt was self-

6

sufficient in food but with a soaring population, wheat and other supplies have had to be imported. The earliest cereals found in Egypt are from the Faiyum and date to c. 4500 B.C. However, this does not necessarily indicate the earliest agriculture, as it is more than likely there are older settlements as yet undiscovered.

The alluvial soil is of two kinds; that near the river being of the better quality, the other a poorer marginal soil on the desert edge. In ancient Egypt, irrigation was carried on by the basin system. This meant the flood water seeped onto the land, which had previously been divided into basins by earthen walls. The higher land was irrigated by means of a *shaduf*, a bucket and counterpoise which could lift water at least ten metres in various stages. These are now being replaced by motorized pumps. When the water had been drained off the basins and they had dried enough, they were ploughed with wooden ploughs similar to those still in use today. Seeds were dropped behind the plough by hand from a leather bag, then flocks of sheep were driven over the ground to tamp in the seeds. Scenes of this being done are portrayed in various Old Kingdom tomb paintings, as at Sheykh Said near el-Amarna.

The grain was cut by flint and later by copper sickles; only the ears were cut, the rest being left to fertilize the soil. The ears were carried in baskets to the threshing-floor and winnowed by being cast into the air from wooden shovels, again similar to those in use today, and the chaff was carried away by the wind. In Prehistoric times the grain was stored in baskets buried in the sand; later it was put in mud silos with an opening at the top. Models of granaries show circular structures with domed roofs, with the contents being noted by an attendant scribe.

Since the introduction of perennial irrigation, the farmers are continuously watering their land, despite water being scarce. This causes widespread drainage difficulties and has led to the rise of subsoil water, which has a deleterious effect on the crops. The monuments are also adversely affected, due to the constant damp which leaches the salt from the stone.

CROPS - The two main crops were barley and wheat. Barley *(Hordoum vulgare)* was the most important as it was used as both animal fodder and for human consumption. It was also the medium of exchange before currency. Wheat, not as salt resistant, was more sparsely grown. This was emmer wheat (*Triticum monococcum*). Yeast was used for fermentation and a yeast fungus (*Saccharomyes winlocki*) has been identified in some of the tombs. Beer, a favourite drink in ancient times, was made from half-baked bread broken up, with water poured on it and allowed to ferment. A similar method is used by the Nubians today when making Bouza, their local beer. Many examples of bread, made from both barley and wheat, have been found in the tombs and there are a number of these loaves in the Egyptian Museum in Cairo.

Pulses, still an important food crop, have been known since early times. Herbs include thyme, mint, fenugreek, liquorice and marjoram. Rice was introduced by the Arabs and is now a major food crop grown in the Delta. Several species of cotton appear to have been native to Egypt, such as tree cotton (*Gossypium aboreum*), which is a perennial plant growing in the southern part of Upper Egypt. The cotton it produces is small and of inferior quality. The short staple cotton *(Gossypium herbaceum)* may be indigenous or have originated in the Sudan where cotton grows wild. It is also found in India and called Asiatic cotton, which is thought to have developed from several hybrid varieties. The main variety of cotton, introduced from America, is the long staple cotton (*Gossypium barbadense*). It is Egypt's main export crop and is grown in Upper Egypt, almost entirely replacing flax which used to be the chief crop, and was used for producing linen in ancient times. Unfortunately, cotton is very prone to boll and cotton worms. An important fodder crop introduced by the Persians in the fifth century B.C. is berseem or Egyptian lucerne clover. It is grown as an infiller, and planted between the summer and winter crops, being usually sown in October. It is the main fodder for donkeys, horses and camels.

VEGETABLES - Favourite vegetables in Egypt, ancient and modern, were onions and garlic. Three types of onion were cultivated, one, at least, of which was indigenous. Lettuce, shown in tomb paintings as offerings, is still widely grown as is celery, which is both a vegetable and a symbol of sorrow. A celery garland was

8

found on the neck of a mummy and can be seen in the Agricultural Museum in Cairo. Cabbage seems to have been introduced in the Ptolemaic Period and grows to a large size, as do cauliflowers. Potatoes, introduced in the last century, are widely cultivated and used as a catch crop to obtain foreign currency. There are two main crops: the winter one planted in November and the summer one planted in February. The latter yields four to five tons per feddan (1 feddan = 1.038 acres). Maize or Indian corn was introduced in the nineteenth century and is grown for animal fodder. Corn meal is grown for human consumption mainly in Upper Egypt, and a certain amount of maize oil is produced. Millet is also grown and is an important food grain. Lentils are widely used for soup and as a vegetable, and are grown in Upper Egypt. Soups are often flavoured with mallow *(Arabic melokhia),* which is also used to accompany pigeon and rabbit. Sugar cane, a major crop, was brought in by the Arabs after their conquest of Egypt in the seventh century A.D. After being pressed, the cane is used to fuel the local sugar factories and gives off a thick black smoke.

TREES Egypt has always had trouble in getting enough timber for its needs, as there are no natural forests. Trees native to Egypt are the Egyptian willow *(Salis subserrta),* the tamarisk *(Tamarisk nilotica),* the siddar *(Zizipus spins-christi),* the balaona *(Balanites aeglptica),* the Nile acacia *(Acacia nilotica),* the moringa *(Moringa peregrina),* the last two being oil producers. A tree that is not indigenous but which has been cultivated from the First Dynasty onwards is the sycamore fig *(Ficus sycomorus)* which came from Arabia and Somaliland. The most valuable wood was imported. This was mainly cedar from the Lebanon and ebony from tropical Africa. Other imported woods were ash, beech, cypress, elm, juniper, lime, liquid amber, maple, oak, pine and yew.

Many of the trees and plants grown in modern Egypt were introduced in the Middle Ages or in the last century. Most fruit trees were unknown in the Pharaonic Period, many being introduced under the Ptolemies. The major types of fruit cultivated at present are citrus. Although known in ancient times, the small fruited lime arrived in the tenth century A.D. and is still widely grown. Orange, lemon, mandarin (known as Yussef Effendi's, from the man who introduced them) and grapefruit were all brought in during the nineteenth century. The mango, now widely grown, was introduced after the Arab conquest. The banana first appeared in the fifth century A.D. Casuarines and eucalyptus, natives of Australia, are now planted as windbreaks along the canals. The white mulberry, grown in the Delta, was introduced in the Byzantine Period when silk-caterpillars were first smuggled in from China. Hence Egypt became a major silk producer in the Middle Ages. The vine was cultivated from Prehistoric times onwards and wine is still produced today.

Three different palms grow in Egypt, each with a special use. The dom palm (*Hyphaene thebaica*), which as its name suggests, grows in Upper Egypt, as far north as Abydos. It is a fan palm, with a branched stem and large, sweet, hard nuts, good for making drinks. The kernel is used for making ornaments while the trunk is hollowed out for water channels. The agum palm (*Medemia argun*) was thought to be extinct until some specimens were found in the oases at Dunkil and Nakila near Kurkur; the violet fruits are inedible but when buried develop a sweetish taste and are shown as food offerings in tomb paintings. The agum is also a fan palm but unbranched. The most useful of the palms is the date palm (*Phoenix dactylifer*). It is unknown in its wild state, but has been present in Egypt since the beginning of recorded history. The date palm needs artificial pollination and this was probably practised by the Egyptians from the Old Kingdom onwards. Pollinating by hand requires special expertise. One man manages a small stand of trees and is paid with a bunch from each tree. The dry variety of date comes from the Aswan area whereas the sweet one is grown in the Giza province. There are thirty different kinds of date varying from dry to sweet. The palm has many uses, apart from its edible dates: matting is made from the leaves and baskets from the fronds, while the trunks serve as roof supports when laid horizontally.

FAUNA - The fauna of Egypt has changed considerably since ancient times. The desert, which used to be full of wildlife, has been decimated by the high velocity rifle and motorized transport; many gazelles, antelopes and oryx that once inhabited the country have now vanished. Tropical animals, once indigenous to Egypt are

10

now extinct. Baboons, sacred to Thoth, the God of Wisdom, no longer occur so far north, nor do apes. Giraffes were portrayed in the desert rock paintings but do not appear in historic times. Hippopotami were once common in the river but are not depicted in wall paintings after the Old Kingdom; occasional ones were seen at Aswan in the late eighteenth century A.D. and there was a hippopotamus goddess, Taweret, who protected women in childbirth. Lions, judging by the records of Amenhotep III, who hunted them in large numbers, seem to have been common up to the middle of the Eighteenth Dynasty. The goddess Sekhmet, who was lion-headed, had her cult centre at Memphis. Jackals and hyenas are common, and in historic times the jackal god, Anubis, was connected with embalming. Wolves, according to naturalists, are unknown in Egypt but the local population is firmly convinced they exist.

The dung beetle or sacred scarab (*Scarabeus sacer*) was regarded as self-created and therefore divine. It was associated with the sun because of its habit of pushing its ball of dung in front of it, and was portrayed as the sun god, Kephre, who was supposed to assist the ball of the sun at its rising. Crocodiles were a menace until the building of the first barrage in the nineteenth century. To placate them, there was a crocodile god, Sobek, who was worshipped at Kom Ombo and in the Faiyum. Perhaps the best-known snake in Egypt is the cobra which appears protecting the king on his head-dress, known as the *uraeus*. The cobra goddess, Wadjet, of Lower Egypt, was one of the primary deities of the country and had her cult centre at Buto, the Predynastic capital of Egypt. There are four other poisonous snakes, the viper being found in the desert and rocky places.

DOMESTIC ANIMALS - Camels, although common now, were not known before the Ptolemaic and Roman times. The first camel-keeping people were the Blemys, who raided Egypt from Nubia during the Roman Period and whose camels are portrayed on many temples. Horses appeared in the Hyksos Period; before this wheeled vehicles did not occur in Egypt and all heavy materials had to be pulled on sledges by hand. Goats probably came in from Asia. Sheep were native to Western Asia. In the Old Kingdom they had horizontal horns *(Ovis longipes)*; they became extinct by the Middle Kingdom and were replaced by *Ovis Amun*. The sheep seen today are the fat-tailed type, common throughout the Middle East; they can live off their tails as camels can live off their humps. There were several ram gods, the most important of which was Khnum, associated with the First Cataract, who created mankind on his potter's wheel. Cattle played an important part in the economy and cattle counts were kept from the beginning of Egyptian history. The cattle suffered severely from plague and had constantly to be renewed, which led to the introduction of the water buffalo in the Middle Ages. The buffalo has a high milk yield and its meat is good to eat. There was a cow goddess, Hathor, whose temple is at Denderah, also bull cults: the Apis bull at Memphis and the Mnevis at Heliopolis. Donkeys are native to the Nile valley and were domesticated early on and used as beasts of burden. The word 'donkey' is still regarded as a term of abuse by the peasants. Another animal that was domesticated early was the dog. Hunting dogs with collars are depicted on the slate palettes at the beginning of the historic period. Later in the Middle Kingdom, Salukis and a type of terrier were shown on the wall paintings. The origin of the present pariah dog is uncertain, but they are unusually gentle animals compared to other breeds found in surrounding countries. Cats appear from Neolithic times onwards. They were traditionally domesticated in Egypt; there was a cat goddess, Bastet, whose cult centre was at Tell Bastat in the Delta. Bees were also domesticated from an early period. The bee is the symbol of Lower Egypt. In Middle Egypt bees are kept, not in hives, but in stacks of drain pipes, a method also used in Ancient Egypt, as shown in Saite tomb paintings on the West Bank at Luxor. Until the introduction of sugar cane, honey was the only means of sweetening. As well as being kept for food, animals and birds used to be bred for temple sacrifices.

BIRDS - Egypt is one of the main migration routes between Africa and the north and, therefore, many of the birds seen in spring and autumn are merely visitors. They do not always follow the river but fly over the desert for long stretches, when this is the more direct route. Migrating flocks of white pelicans, white storks and

cranes are a splendid sight. Birds were frequently used as hieroglyphic signs. Several of those shown are now extinct or are no
longer found so far north, such as the sacred ibis, last seen in 1876.
The ibis was sacred to Thoth, the God of Wisdom. Barn owls can
still be seen and closely resemble the owl hieroglyph. The cormor-
ant vanished in 1877. The vulture was the goddess of Upper Egypt
called Nekhbet with her cult centre at Nekheb (el-Kab). Birds were
extensively hunted and still are today; they do not appear to have
been domesticated in ancient times, but today there are large duck
farms in the Khargah Oasis and at Aswan. Geese and ducks breed
in Egypt and some over-winter. The white-fronted goose was
shown in wall paintings as early as the Third Dynasty and was
associated with the earth god, Geb. It is found all over Egypt but is
not so numerous as it was formerly. The white-headed duck winters
in the Delta. The hen is a late-comer; it did not appear from Asia
until after the seventh century B.C. Domestic pigeons, of which
there are four varieties, are extensively kept for eating and for
their manure. Doves include the collared dove and the palm dove.
The ostrich, whose feathers were used for fans, was once plentiful
but is now rarely seen in the surrounding deserts. Cattle egrets
breed extensively and were common from Prehistoric times, where
they were shown on painted Naqada pottery.

FISH - The fish of the Nile used to be very prolific; the two most
important being the Nile perch (*Lates Niloticus*) and the bolti
(*Tilapia Niloticus*). Since the High Dam was built these are mainly
found in Lake Nasser, where the perch grow to a very large size.
The Red Sea is tropical, with coral reefs among which are found
beautiful coral fish, many of the genera are brightly coloured but
there are several poisonous varieties. Moray eels are found there,
and sharks of several species are much in evidence, namely the
tiger shark, the Red Sea lemon shark and the great white shark. In
the Mediterranean, mullet both grey and red are an important
source of food.

HISTORY

The terminology used in Egyptology has always presented a problem. The earliest Egyptologists were classicists so it was natural for them to use Greek terms. Also Manetho, an Egyptian priest, in the third century B.C. wrote an account of the kings' reigns in Greek. Unfortunately his original work has not survived and only fragmentary records are preserved in the later writings of Josephus, Africanus and Eusebius. It was Manetho who divided the Egyptian rulers into dynasties, a practice continued by later Egyptologists, and he gave no reason for adopting this procedure. The division of the reigns into Old, Middle and New Kingdom has been a recent addition.

As well as Manetho, there are other older sources of Egyptian history. The earliest historical inscription is the Palermo Stone, a fragment of black diorite, which records the kings' names and the most important events of their reigns down to the Fifth Dynasty. The Tablet of Karnak, dating from the Eighteenth Dynasty but not arranged in chronological order, contains sixty-one kings' names up until the time of Tuthmosis III. The King List in the temple of Seti I at Abydos gives the order of seventy-six kings from Menes to Seti I, but several dynasties have been omitted such as the Thirteenth to the Seventeenth Dynasties, as well as several kings from the Eighteenth Dynasty. A shorter list, similar but damaged, was found on a block in the temple of Ramesses II at Abydos. The Royal List of Saqqara preserves the cartouches of forty-seven kings starting at the end of the First Dynasty down to Ramesses II. Also the Turin Papyrus, written in hieratic and dated to c. 1200 B.C., gives a list of three hundred names and divides the rulers into dynasties.

The kings' names are complicated and because of the absence of vocalization, in hieroglyphic writing there can be no fixed norm for the transcription of proper names. Thus the name *Ḏḥwty-ḥtp*

King List in the Temple of Seti I at Abydos

is transcribed variously by different writers as Tetuihetep, Thoth-otpu, Thuthotep or Dhuthotpe, leaving the layman to wonder what was intended. In certain cases, some assistance can be obtained from contemporary writing in cuneiform, such as the Boğazköy tablets or the Amarna letters.

The titulary of the king consisted of five names, not all of which came into use at the same time:

1. The Horus name, also called the *Ka* name, written inside a *serekh* and surmounted by a figure of the hawk god Horus.

2. The *nebty* name, meaning the two goddesses of Upper and Lower Egypt: Nekhbet, the vulture goddess and Wadjet, the cobra goddess, who were two of the primeval mother goddesses closely associated with the king.

3. The Golden Horus name, variously explained as showing the victory of Horus over Seth, or indicating a falcon of gold.

Serekh of King Zer from Saqqara

16

4.   The prenomen, given to the king at his coronation, is preceded by the title *n-sw-bt* which means 'he who belongs to the sedge and the bee', the plant and insect symbolizing Upper and Lower Egypt. The prenomen is always compounded with the name Re.

5.   The nomen, introduced by the term *s3 r'*, was the name given to the king at birth, and was the equivalent of a family name. Names 4 and 5 were both written inside a cartouche, the use of which was peculiar to royalty.

The term 'pharaoh' is a title derived from *pr'3*, the Great House, referring to the palace. It does not appear in Egyptian usage until the Twenty-second Dynasty and then as a translation of the respectful term for the Great House rather as the Ottoman Sultan was referred to as the Sublime Porte, the name of his palace in Stanbul.

Queens had an interesting position in Egypt. From the First Dynasty, they were able to hold kingship and through marriage linked different regions together. The connection between the dynasties is almost certainly through the female line, although this is not clearly shown until the reign of Queen Tetisheri in the Eighteenth Dynasty.

The history of Egypt is indissolubly linked with the Nile. The movement of the river and the deposit of its silt has resulted in the virtual disappearance of the prehistoric settlements, leaving only cemetery sites on the edge of the desert escarpment. This survival of the cemeteries rather than the village and later town sites is a marked feature of Egyptian archaeology and tends to give a somewhat disproportionate emphasis to the funerary aspect of Egyptian culture.

LANGUAGE - Until the discovery of the Rosetta Stone at Rashid in the Western Delta in 1798, which is now in the British Museum, it had not been possible to read the hieroglyphic writing of Ancient Egypt. The inscription on the stone is a copy of a decree issued in Memphis in 196 B.C. by a priestly council in honour of King Ptolemy V Epiphanes (203-181 B.C.). It was written in three scripts and two languages: Egyptian hieroglyphs, Egyptian demotic and Greek. The Greek text was easy to read and it was not long before the names of the Ptolemaic rulers were recognized in the demotic text. Thomas Young (1779-1829), an English scientist and the author of *The Undulatory Theory of Light*, recognized that the hieroglyphic script consisted of phonetic signs and that the royal names were written in ovals (cartouches). It is difficult to assess the value of Young's contribution to Jean François Champollion's (1790-1832) discoveries, but by the time of the latter's death the foundation of the decipherment of hieroglyphs had been laid and the Egyptian language ordered - probably made possible by Champollion's knowledge of oriental languages, including Coptic. Following the decipherment, there was a rush to remove as many antiquities as possible from Egypt and there were well organized expeditions by the French, German and Italians to record the extant inscriptions, although it was not until the beginning of this century that the American, Henry Breasted, brought out his list of historical inscriptions.

On examination, it appeared that the Egyptian language was written in various scripts. Hieroglyphic writing is divided into Old Egyptian, Middle Egyptian and Late Egyptian, with considerable variations between the early and late writing when many additional signs were added. Hieratic is a cursive form of hieroglyphs and Demotic is a later cursive form used after 700 B.C. The term hieroglyph comes from the Greek *hieros* meaning sacred and *glypho* meaning sculptured, and is the writing found on temple walls and on public monuments. The hieroglyphic writing consists of phonograms and ideograms, the latter being used at the end of words; vowels were not written as in Semitic languages.

With the conquest of Alexander, the official language became Greek and remained so under the Roman and Byzantine Empires. It was as a result of the conversion to Christianity in the first two centuries A.D. that it was found necessary to develop Coptic as a written language in order to produce a version of the Scriptures in a language intelligible to the people. The Coptic script was developed from the Greek alphabet with certain signs added from Demotic to represent sounds that were not present in Greek letters. This became the official language of Christian Egypt and survived as a spoken language until the sixteenth century, when it was replaced by Arabic. It is still used, together with Arabic in Coptic church services.

18

In the seventh century, Arabic was introduced and gradually became the official language of the country. After the Ottoman invasion of 1517, Turkish became the official language, and it remained the language used in the army until the 1952 revolution.

Today, Arabic is once again the official language of Egypt. There are regional dialects and pronounciations such as the 'j' alternating with the 'g', as in Jebel or Gebel, and common words differ like bread and money. For example, a hoe is called a *tourier* in Upper Egypt and a *fas* in the Delta.

Hieroglyphic

Hieratic

Demotic

Coptic

تعتبر الجيزة من اهم احياء القاهرة الفخمة على الشاطىء الغربى

Arabic

Samples of the various scripts used in the Egyptian language

THE CALENDAR - The Pharaonic year was based on the lunar calendar which had twelve months, each month having three ten-day weeks. At the end of the twelve lunar months, or 360 days, there were five intercalary days on which festivals were held. The months were originally numbered, and were not named until the Persian Period when they were called after the principal religious festivals held during the month. The rising of Sothis or Sirus, the Dog Star, marked the first day of the first month and once in 1,460 years it coincided with the lunar calendar. As the calendar was not exact, after 120 years it was a month out, and an extra month had to be added to the year. When this was first discovered, it was thought by some early Egyptologists, including Sir Flinders Petrie, that the Sothic cycle was in use in the First Dynasty, thus putting back the dates of the dynasty by one thousand years. It is now thought that the Sothic cycle came in later. The agricultural year had three seasons of four months each: the inundation, winter and spring.

It is known that systematic astronomical observance began very early in Egypt. It used to be taken on the roofs of temples. The orientation of religious buildings was important to the Egyptians and foundation scenes in the temples show that the structure was begun by taking astral observations. Texts found on coffin lids as early as the Ninth Dynasty refer to star clocks and give the name of the thirty-six decans (stars which rose at ten day intervals at the same time as the sun). Similar star charts were found on the ceilings of tombs of the New Kingdom, such as that of Senmut, Hatshepsut's architect and steward, the Osireion at Abydos, and in the tombs of Ramesses IV, Ramesses VII and Ramesses IX. The object of these star charts was to enable the dead man to tell the time of the night and the date of the calendar.

The Egyptians were the first to devise a twenty-four division of the day and night, though the length of the hours varied according to the season. It was the Hellenistic astronomers in Egypt who divided the hour into sixty minutes, a system of Babylonian origin. Julius Caesar introduced the Julian calendar as a result of his contacts with Hellenistic astronomers at Alexandria and observations carried out in Egypt.

20

Prehistoric cultures wherever they occur are rather similar. It is not until people acquire a certain degree of civilization that marked differences appear. The beginnings of Egyptian history are to be found with the unification under the first king, Menes or Mena of the Two Lands in about 3100 B.C. The Two Lands consisted of the Nile Valley and the Delta. This vital division between the two was recognized by the Ancient Egyptians themselves, who spoke of their country as the Two Lands, Upper and Lower Egypt, the Southland and the Northland or Shemau and To-mehu. The struggles that led to the unification between the tribes of the Northland and those of the Southland survived into the historical period, as the legends of the battles of Horus and Seth.

Menes established the first capital at Memphis, not far from modern Cairo. Strategically, this was an excellent position being at the apex of the Delta and at the gateway to Upper Egypt. Memphis became known as 'The White Walls' and was recognized throughout Egyptian history as the symbol of the unity of the country, although it was not always the administrative capital, and for a short period in the First Dynasty, This or Thinis was the capital.

The burial place for Memphis was Saqqara. Or was it? Here one has an anomaly, because the First and Second Dynasty rulers have two burial places: one at Saqqara and one at Abydos, which later became the official burial place of Osiris. Of the two, the one at Saqqara seems to have been the largest and argument has been intense among Egyptologists as to where the kings were actually buried and as to whether one was a cenotaph as opposed to an actual burial place. As both sites have been robbed, the tombs burnt and the bodies missing, it is difficult to say where they were interred, as all this happened centuries before the tombs were examined scientifically. At both Saqqara and Abydos, the kings were accompanied by sacrificed servants, who were buried in subsidiary tombs round the main panelled mud-brick tomb. This practice ceased after the Second Dynasty and was replaced in the Fourth Dynasty by model servants being buried and later in the Twelfth Dynasty by the *shabti* figures, which were made first in wax and clay, and then in faience. They were supposed, by means of magic, to be revived so as to be able to work for their masters in the After World.

The possibility that Abydos was the actual burial place is suggested by the presence of an arm with bracelets on it, found bricked up in the wall of Zer's tomb there. This would seem to indicate that his queen, at least, had been buried at Abydos. Another factor to be considered, is the curious practice of Egyptian multiple burials which continue down to the present day. This can be seen in the burials of holy men or sheikhs who have several tombs, which suggests that the real tomb may be at el-Kab with others at Aswan, Tanta and Abydos. Offerings are made to all these and the faithful behave as though there was a body present in each tomb.

THE ARCHAIC PERIOD

For the first two dynasties, in addition to the king lists, there is contemporary evidence in the shape of ornamental palettes, mace-heads and ivory labels inscribed with scenes representing historical events at the beginning of Egyptian history. However, these are fragmentary and difficult to interpret. What is certain is that from c. 3100 B.C., Egypt had a centralized government with power centred in the king, who had semi-divine status and who served as intercessor between his people and the gods.

The rapid development that took place in Egypt after the unification of the Two Lands is almost certainly due to the introduction of irrigation. Evidence for this is to be seen on the Scorpion mace-head found at Hierakonpolis. This has three registers: the first depicts dead birds hanging from the standards of the Southern confederacy showing the conquest of the North by the South. The middle register shows King Scorpion excavating a canal amid scenes of rejoicing, and the lower one, work on agriculture. The mace-head symbolizes the conquest of the North by the South, the subsequent beginnings of irrigation and finally the united land settling down to work in the fields.

Among the most interesting of these documents is the Narmer Palette commemorating a king who ruled at the time of the unification and whose two sides depict the conquering king, first wear-

22

ing the White Crown of the South, and on the other side, the Red Crown of the North. Narmer's mace-head shows him enthroned, wearing the Red Crown and protected by the vulture goddess, Nekhbet. In front of him is a woman in a carrying-chair who may well be the Northern heiress Neith-hotep, whom he married to consolidate the Two Lands.

Neith-hotep was buried in a splendid mud-brick tomb at Naqada, which was as large and imposing as any king's; her northern tomb was probably at Helwan. Narmer, by comparison, was buried in a comparatively small tomb at Abydos; his main tomb, which is possibly at Saqqara or Tarkhan, has not been found. Their son was Horus Aha, almost certainly to be equated with Mena, the first king of the First Dynasty.

Little is known of the eight kings of this dynasty save their names. Not all their tombs have been found and few events are known from their reigns, except that Mena ruled for sixty years and was carried off by a hippopotamus. Even less is known of the nine kings of the Second Dynasty. The first was Hotepsekhemwy, c. 2890 B.C. Under the second king, the worship of the Apis and Mnevis bulls was introduced and under the third, Nynetjer, it was confirmed that women might hold the kingly office. There was apparently a struggle for power at the end of the dynasty, as under the last king, Khasekhemwy, the emblems of both Horus and Seth appear on the *serekh*. Khasekhemwy was a remarkable king who reigned for thirty years. He appears to have reunited the Two Lands and his achievements paved the way for the Third Dynasty. His queen, Nyma'athap, was regarded as the ancestress of the Third Dynasty.

THE OLD KINGDOM (c. 2686-2181 B.C.)

This early dynastic period was the time during which the basis of Egyptian civilization was firmly established. Writing advanced and became more flexible, and techniques in craft and industry developed. Stone replaced brick and many of the architectural forms that are found throughout the historic period now appear. The king under whom these changes took place was Djoser, and it was in his reign that the Step Pyramid was built. This was the first building built wholly of stone, for although stone had been used in certain structures before, this was an entirely new development. The use of limestone in the Step Pyramid complex showed a remarkable mastery of material and was far in advance of anything seen previously. It was built by Imhotep, Djoser's chief of works. Djoser is also known to have sent expeditions to Sinai in search of copper, turquoise and lapis lazuli. It seems likely that it was in his reign that the southern boundary of Egypt was fixed at Elephantine, and that from the Third Dynasty onwards, the country had a highly centralized administration.

The Old Kingdom is sometimes dated from the Fourth Dynasty, and this is slightly better documented as its rulers are known more from their material remains than anything else. Pyramids proliferate at Dahshur, Giza and Abu Roash. These pyramids were built during the inundation, when the land was flooded and the peasants idle, never by slave labour. Herodotus has suggested that a work force of 100,000 was employed, but this would have been unwieldy and American engineers have since calculated that not more than 4,000 men would have been required, including those engaged in quarrying the stone at Aswan and elsewhere, and those who ferried the blocks to the site. It is estimated that the Great Pyramid at Giza contained some 2,300,000 blocks of stone. Trade was carried out with Byblos, and Snefru is known to have sent expeditions there to get cedar wood for his pyramids at Dahshur. Snefru had a reputation for being a good king. The same cannot be said of the builders of the pyramids at Giza, Khufu and Khafre, who were not well thought of.

Administration was largely in the hands of the royal family and they held most of the main offices of state. During the Fifth Dynasty, some modification took place in the king's status and for the first time, the king is referred to as the Son of Re. The first three kings claimed descent from the sun god, according to a legend current during the Middle Kingdom. During the Fifth Dynasty, smaller pyramids were built and at the end of the period, the tomb chambers were inscribed with the Pyramid Texts, which were complicated, religious texts telling of the king's ascent to the After World. This practice continued in the Sixth Dynasty.

24

During the long reign of Pepi II, who was thought to have reigned for about ninety-four years, the central power gradually diminished and finally collapsed. This led to the decentralization of the government and to the rise to power of the provincial governors or nomarchs. This was followed by a series of low Niles, and Egypt lapsed into chaos, which led to what is called the First Intermediate Period. The country was divided and there was a struggle for power between the warring dynasts. The south gained ascendancy and the land was reunited under Nebhepetre Mentuhotpe II of Thebes, who took the Horus name of Smatowy 'He who unites the Two Lands'. Thus began the period known as the Middle Kingdom.

THE MIDDLE KINGDOM (c. 2050-1786 B.C.)

Nothing is known of the way Mentuhotpe restored power, but he continued to consolidate Egypt's frontiers by raids against the Nubians and Libyans. By the end of his long reign, Egypt was in a better position than she had been for years. The foundations of the Middle Kingdom were firmly established, both politically and artistically. Mentuhotpe built a splendid tomb at the foot of the Libyan hills at Deir el-Bahari on the West Bank at Thebes. This was the precursor of the many royal tombs to be built there. It was under the kings of the following dynasty, the Twelfth, that Egypt became once more a well organized country with a definite home and foreign policy. The control of Nubia was established by a series of fortresses, combined with trading posts, through which the products of Nubia and places further to the south reached the Egyptian market. These fortresses were remarkable, and embodied many technical features not seen again until the medieval period in Europe. The nomarchs were a problem. They had become much too powerful and were subdued by Amenemhat II and Senusert III. During this period, the capital was moved from Thebes to Itj-Towy (Lisht), just to the north of the Faiyum, from where the Two Lands could be more easily controlled. There was considerable trade with Western Asia, particularly with the Lebanon and Syria, from whence much of the timber needed by Egypt was obtained. It was at this time that the defensive walls known as the 'Walls of the Prince' were built to keep out the waves of Asiatics who tried to infiltrate the Delta from the east.

THE SECOND INTERMEDIATE PERIOD (1786-1567 B.C.)

The time between the end of the Twelfth Dynasty and the rise of the Eighteenth Dynasty is usually known as the Second Intermediate Period. Manetho assigned five dynasties to this time. Again, weakness of the central government afforded an opportunity for the Asiatics to infiltrate the eastern Delta. These Asiatics were called the Hyksos, and they established a separate kingdom in northern Egypt centred on their capital at Avaris, the location of which is still disputed. Little is known of the Hyksos: where they came from or what their name means, although it has been suggested it meant 'rulers of foreign countries' or 'shepherd kings'. While the Hyksos were ruling in the north, an Egyptian dynasty was ruling at Thebes and in the Seventeenth Dynasty, it made a determined effort to get rid of the Hyksos and restore power to the Egyptians. However, they did not succeed completely until the beginning of the Eighteenth Dynasty.

THE NEW KINGDOM (1567-1085 B.C.)

The New Kingdom consisted of three dynasties, the Eighteenth, Nineteenth and Twentieth. It is impossible to mention all the kings of this period; the beginning was marked by a series of strong, able and energetic rulers who traced their descent from Queen Tetisheri, the royal ancestress of the Eighteenth Dynasty. The first king, Ahmose, was occupied in driving out the Hyksos and consolidating his position. Not only did he defeat them in Egypt but he followed them into Asia and destroyed their stronghold at Sharuhen in Southern Palestine, after a three year siege. His expansionist policy marked the beginning of the New Kingdom, which is sometimes called the Empire. This empire extended at its widest limits from Napata in the Sudan to the river Euphrates in Syria. Syria and Palestine consisted of a large number of city states with whom Egypt had a series of treaties and put garrisons

26

at key points to keep order. The tenure was insecure and every time an Egyptian ruler died there were repeated revolts. This was also a time of periodic empire building by the Hittites, which ressulted with first one power dominating the area then the other.

The Eighteenth Dynasty from 1567-1320 B.C. is usually considered one of the most important periods in Egyptian history and most observations made about ancient Egypt are based on monuments and information derived from this time. One of the most interesting rulers was Hatshepsut (1503-1482 B.C.) whose mortuary temple at Deir el-Bahari is one of the masterpieces of Egyptian architecture, comparable only to the Step Pyramid complex at Saqqara. It was built by her architect, Senmut. Hatshepsut was the wife of Tuthmosis II who died after a brief reign. She was the Great Royal Heiress and claimed that her father Tuthmosis I had crowned her king of Egypt, so that after the death of her husband she assumed the kingship. Until recently, it was thought her reign was a period of consolidation but recent research has shown that she personally campaigned in both Nubia and Syria. She also sent an expedition to Punt (Somalia) for incense, which is depicted on the walls of her mortuary temple. Hatshepsut is noted for her revival of Egyptian art which for the first few reigns of the dynasty was stiff and unbending.

Another great king of the dynasty was Tuthmosis III, the general who led the Egyptian army as far as the Euphrates, and who established a series of vassal states in Syria, the Lebanon and Palestine. The sons of the Asiatic princes were taken as hostages to Egypt and educated at the Egyptian court, where together with the young Nubian chieftans, they became thoroughly Egyptianized. During the period when these rulers and their sons were in power, Egypt had little trouble in Asia but towards the end of the dynasty, the strong line of Egyptian kings began to weaken and Amenhotep III is noted more for his vast building programmes in Egypt and Nubia than for any active foreign policy.

His son Amenhotep IV, better known as Akhenaten, was a religious reformer, who fell out with the priests of Amun at Thebes and moved to Akhetaten (modern el-Amarna) in Middle Egypt, where he established a capital as far away as he could from the hostile priesthood. It collapsed on his death, seventeen years later.

27

Akhenaten has been the subject of much speculation; he was regarded by some Egyptologists as one of the first monotheists. However, it is unlikely now that anyone would regard him in this light. He preferred the worship of Aten to that of Amun-Re, the Theban god. Aten was a very old Heliopolitan god, who represented the beneficial rays of the sun, so that Akhenaten did not, in fact, introduce a new religion but only modified an existing one. The art of the Amarna period has been much praised for its realistic portrayals, particularly of the royal family, but it is a degenerate art, and the repeated portraits of the king and his beautiful wife, Nefertiti, replacing as they do to a large extent the normal tomb paintings, those in the tombs at Amarna give us a less clear picture of everyday life at Akhetaten than does the art in the Theban necropolis.

The cause of the death of Akhenaten is uncertain. His body has not been found, although he was almost certainly buried at Akhetaten. His co-regent Smenkhare, disappears almost at the same time, but was buried at Thebes and his body was found in an unnamed sarcophagus in Tomb 55 in the Valley of the Kings. After this, Akhetaten was abandoned and the royal family returned to Thebes and Memphis. During the reign of Akhenaten the Egyptian Empire in Western Asia gradually disintegrated. Whether the letters from the princes of the city states found at el-Amarna were ever seen by Akhenaten, or ever answered, we do not know, but no body of troups was sent to support the few vassal States that remained loyal in Asia and gradually they too were overthrown. The letters from Tunip in North Syria are particularly moving. Part of letter 59 says:

> "And now for twenty years, we have been sending to the
>   king, our lord . . .
> But now Tunip,
> Your city weeps,
> And her tears are running
> And there is no help for us".

The king who followed Akhenaten, was the boy king, Tutankhamun, well-known for the discovery of his almost intact tomb in

1922 by Lord Carnarvon and Howard Carter. He reigned for about ten years and died from a blow which fractured his skull. Whether he was murdered or received the wound accidently is impossible to say. Under Tutankhamun, the worship of Amun was restored and the temples of Amun renovated. Whether this was the will of the young king or his advisors is uncertain. When he died, aged about eighteen, he was buried with considerable splendour in a tomb, that had not been intended for him, in the Valley of the Kings. The magnificent jewellery, the gold shrines, furniture and ornaments found with this rather obscure king of the Eighteenth Dynasty is an indication of the considerable wealth of the New Kingdom rulers. His death marks the end of the legitimate royal house of the Eighteenth Dynasty. The last two kings of the dynasty, Ay and Horemheb, were not of royal blood, although one may have married one of the royal heiresses. The attempt made by Ankhesenamun, the widow of Tutankhamun, to obtain a Hittite prince as a husband, and his murder soon after crossing the Egyptian frontier, hints at problems over the accession of which we are only dimly aware. The plague that swept over Egypt and Hatti (the Hittite Empire), at the end of the Eighteenth Dynasty, only weakened the country further.

The Nineteenth Dynasty shows a renewal of Egyptian military power. The first king Ramesses, an Egyptian general, reigned for only a few years. His son, Seti I, left splendid monuments at Abydos and his tomb on the West Bank, and he restored Egyptian power in Western Asia. His son, Ramesses II, had one of the longest reigns in Egypt, and is perhaps best known for his battle against the Hittites and the league of Syrian States, which culminated in the indecisive battle of Kadesh, which he extensively portrayed on his many temples. He was also well-known for his building works but in order to do this he robbed earlier monuments and his work does not show the artistry and good taste of his father. In sculpture particularly, more has survived from his reign than any other, although some of the pieces marked with his name are usurped from earlier rulers. He built extensively, not only in Egypt, but throughout Nubia, a series of splendid rock-cut temples, now largely flooded, with the exception of Abu Simbel and Beit el-Wali. By the end of his long reign, the creative force of the Nineteenth Dynasty rulers had largely expended itself. His son, Merneptah, was already a middle-aged man by the time he ascended the throne and was best known for his defeat of the Libyans in a series of battles and his mention of the Israelites on a stele found in his temple on the West Bank.

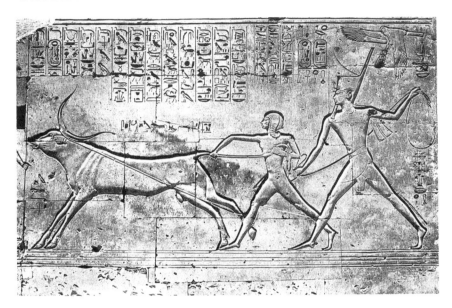

Ramesses II with his son Prince Hirkhopshef throwing the bull at Abydos

The Egyptians won the war against the Sea Peoples and the Libyans under Ramesses III, but lost their Empire in Asia and with it their source of iron, the new metal that was to revolutionize life in the first millennium B.C. Unfortunately for them, they did not know of the vast iron resources within the African continent included in their sphere of influence, on the Nile near Meroe, Aswan and the Bahriyah Oasis. The exhaustion of the gold mines in the Wadi Allaqi and other gold mines in the eastern desert, also presaged difficulties for Egypt. She was no longer the richest country in the ancient world and could not afford the mercenary armies she had employed in the times of the Eighteenth and Nineteenth Dynasties. It is known that there was bubonic plague in the Egyptian forces at the end of the Eighteenth Dynasty, as they introduced it into the Hittite Empire. It is also known that there was a

severe smallpox epidemic in the later years of the reign of Ramesses III. These two diseases must have taken their toll of the dep-
leted Egyptian manpower, already exhausted by their continual
struggles against the Sea Peoples and the Libyans. The other cause
of the decay of Egyptian power was the over-spending by the
royal house on the temples and estates of Amun, which led to the
disruption of the balance of power in Egypt itself. The later kings
of the Nineteenth and Twentieth Dynasties, with the exception of
Ramesses III, who built a splendid mortuary temple, where his
victories against the Sea Peoples and Libyans were recorded, were
largely nonentities.

THE THIRD INTERMEDIATE PERIOD (1085-332 B.C.)

The period after 1085 B.C., from the end of the Twentieth Dynasty, is sometimes called the Third Intermediate Period and
Egypt goes into a long, slow decline. For a short time there was a
revival in the Twenty-Second Dynasty, when warrior kings carried
Egyptian arms back into Palestine, in the fifth year of Rehoboam,
King of Judah. The capital moved from Thebes to various places in
the Delta, and the Kushite, Twenty-fifth Dynasty, was no match
for the Assyrians when they invaded Egypt in 667 B.C. They
sacked, first, Memphis in that year and then Thebes in 663 B.C. A
brief revival occurred under the Twenty-sixth, or Saite, Dynasty
when Egypt turned towards Greece and employed large numbers
of Greek mercenaries. However, Necho (610-597 B.C.) was defeated near Carchemish on the Euphrates by Nebuchadrezzar of Babylon, and was forced to withdraw back to his own frontier. Greek
influence was shown by the foundation of Naukratis as a Greek
trading city in the Delta.
    The end of this dynasty was brought about by the Persian
invasion of 525 B.C. under Cambyses. He became the first king of
the Twenty-seventh Dynasty and for the next two centuries Egypt
was largely under Persian rule as one of its satrapies. After a brief
period in the fourth century, the Twenty-ninth and Thirtieth
Dynasties, Egypt regained its independence until the Persians again
invaded the country under Artaxerxes III in 343 B.C. For the next
ten years, the Persians held the country which finally fell to Alex-

ander, with hardly a blow, after the battle of Issus in 333 B.C. Alexander visited Egypt and consulted the oracle of Amun in the Siwa Oasis and assumed the trappings of divinity. On his death he was buried in Egypt. Though the whereabouts of his grave is unknown, it would have been almost certainly in Alexandria, the city which he founded. Alexander appointed Ptolemy Soter, his favourite general, to govern Egypt and it was he who founded the Ptolemaic Dynasty, which ruled Egypt for the next three hundred years with considerable ability.

THE PTOLEMAIC PERIOD (332-30 B.C.)

Egypt now became part of the Hellenistic world, and the establishment of the Mouseion and Library at Alexandria made her one of the greatest seats of Hellenistic learning. The Ptolemies built up the Egyptian navy and endeavoured to identify themselves with the interests of their Egyptian subjects. With this in mind, they built extensive temples and monuments and allowed themselves to be worshipped by their subjects as divinities, thus carrying on the old Egyptian idea of the divine kingship. The last of the Ptolemies was Cleopatra, a queen much misrepresented by Shakespeare. She was, in fact, an able administrator and wished to restore Egypt to its former glory. However, the rising power of Rome, the evident weakness of the later Ptolemies and the wealth of Egypt, led to its annexation by Rome in 30 B.C., following the deaths of Cleopatra and Anthony after their unsuccessful bid to become the leaders of the Eastern Empire.

THE ROMAN AND BYZANTINE EMPIRES (30 B.C.-A.D. 642)

Egypt, first under the Romans and then under the Byzantines, went through a chequered period. After the first two centuries of Roman rule, when Egypt had been comparatively prosperous, the Roman provincial system started to decline. Egypt had been the granary of the Roman Empire until the reign of Commodus (A.D. 190-192), when Egyptian supplies had to be supplemented from North Africa, and the coinage was debased. Until the time of Diocletian, all the troops were organized as a single force under the command of the Prefect and based at Alexandria, Pelusium, Babylon, Koptos, Thebes and Syene (Aswan). An attempt was made to control part of Nubia but later the frontier was withdrawn to the First Cataract and a line of forts were set up, linking Philae to Syene.

It was Diocletian (A.D. 284-305) who ceased to administer Egypt as a separate province and assimilated it into the Eastern Empire. Egypt came under the Prefect of the East and was split into three provinces: the Thebaid, Aegyptus Jovia and Aegyptus Herculia. About 341, a fresh province, named Augustus, was formed and by the fourth century, Herculia was renamed Arcadia, and all the provinces were sub-divided into two. At the same time, the position of the prefect in charge of the area diminished and civil and military power was split into two. The local system of dating by the regnal year of the emperor, and the use of separate local coinage was suspended and replaced by that in general use throughout the Empire. This system remained more or less unchanged until the Arab invasion of A.D. 642.

The Egyptians were not better off under the Byzantines than they had been under the Romans; all that happened was that the grain ships went to Constantinople instead of Rome. The official capital of Egypt was still Alexandria, as it had been during the whole of the Ptolemaic and Roman Periods. The tax system was simplified but was still as onerous as before. Under Constantine I (A.D. 323-337), the official recognition of Christianity, far from establishing peace in the province, led to further trouble between the Greek Orthodox Church and the Egyptian Coptic Church. Matters were not eased by the accession of the pagan emperor, Julian, in 361. The country was racked, not only by religious strife and political schisms, but by internal revolts and the invasion of the Blemmyes into Egypt from Nubia, where they ranged almost unchecked in the south of the country. There was a change too in the armed forces; by the fifth century, all the Roman Legions had gone from Egypt and were largely replaced by local levies with garrisons in the larger towns and principal forts. These garrisons were sufficient for police duties but were not strong enough to repel any serious invasion.

This was the position when Heraclius I (A.D. 610-641) became Emperor. Six years later, the Persians of the Sassanian Dynasty invaded Egypt, sacked Alexandria and massacred its inhabitants. They then advanced into Middle and Upper Egypt leaving a trail of devastation behind them. They controlled the country for about ten years, that is until 626, when they were then defeated in Syria and Mesopotamia by Heraclius, who restored Byzantine rule, and once again set up his garrisons in Egypt.

Before things had time to settle down, a new danger appeared for the Byzantines with the eruption of Arab forces emerging from Arabia under the impetus of their newly-developed Islamic religion. The Byzantines were defeated, first at Gabatha and then at Yarmuk in 634. Damascus fell the following year and Heraclius was a broken man, when he retreated first to Antioch and later to Constantinople in 636.

ARAB EGYPT

The Arab invasion of Egypt in A.D. 639 came across the Sinai Desert and advanced through Pelusium and Bilbeis, where strong resistance delayed them. They finally attacked the fort of Babylon, situated in what is now, old Cairo. It took seven months to capture, partly due to the Arabs diverting part of their army on an unsuccessful expedition to the Faiyum. Reinforcements of twelve thousand men arrived to assist the Amir, Amr ibn el-As, the general in command of the Arab forces. On the 6th April 641, Babylon capitulated.

Amr made his headquarters at Fustat (the Encampment), a new town built near the ruins of a Roman fort, on the orders of Khalif 'Umar. This became the administrative centre of Egypt instead of the old capital of Alexandria.

At first, Egypt was under the Khalifate of Mecca, but as time went by the power of the Khalifate declined, due to dynastic quarrels, and with the appointment of Ahmad ibn Talun as governor in 868, Egypt became virtually independent. He moved the capital to a new town, north-west of Fustat, called el-Qatar (the Concessions), raised a large army of slaves and built extensively, including the mosque which still bears his name today. Before his death in 884,

34

he controlled much of Syria. The dynasty he started ended after only three rulers, and in 905, the Abbasid forces from Baghdad invaded the country and for the next thirty years Egypt was ruled by governors appointed by Baghdad. From 935-969, it was more or less independent under the governorship of the Ikhshids. 'Ikhshid' was a Persian title meaning ruler and was given to Muhammad ibn Tughj, the first of the Ikhshid Dynasty, who retained friendly relations with Baghdad.

THE FATIMIDS (A.D. 969-1171)

The Ikhshids were followed by the Fatimids, who claimed descent from Fatimah, the daughter of the Prophet Muhammad, and who were Shi'i Muslims. A group of them, followers of the Seventh Imam, Ismail, came from Syria in 909 and settled in North Africa, in what is now Tunisia. Their aim was the conquest of Baghdad and the possession of the Khalifate. They had attacked Egypt several times during the Ikhshid regime, without success. It was not until after a series of low Niles and famines that they succeeded in their ambitions in 969, when led by Jahwar. Having captured Fustat, they immediately started to build a new city for the Khalif al-Mu'izz, called al-Qahirah (the Victorious). The empire of the Fatimids was enormous, stretching over North Africa, Sicily, Egypt and the Hejaz to North Syria, and they had a vast army of slaves taken from many countries. During the last two reigns, the power of the army commanders increased and they became the ruling force in the empire. The administration, however, broke down after a bit and a series of famines once again led to chaos. The Khalif sent for the Governor of Acre, Badr al-Jamali, to take control. Order was restored and he was soon master of Egypt. Badr was succeeded by his son and then a series of Amirs. In 1077, North Syria, which was controlled by the Seljuk Turks, disintegrated into a series of feuding states and the situation became even more complicated by the arrival of the First Crusade in 1097.

The Christians wished to set up states of their own, centred on Jerusalem. This they achieved when they captured Jerusalem in 1099. The Crusaders attacked Egypt in 1168, and Nur al-Din, the Sultan of Syria, sent his Kurdish commander, Shirkuh, to Egypt to help the Fatimids repel the Christians. Shirkuh became Wazir to the Fatimid, Khalif al-Adid, but died soon afterwards. He was succeeded by his nephew, Salah al-Din (Saladin), who had accompanied him on his campaign. On the death of al-Adid, Salah al-Din became, to all intents and purposes, an independent ruler, acknowledging the suzerainity in the name of the Khalifs of Baghdad. This was the beginning of the Ayyubid Dynasty.

THE AYYUBIDS (A.D. 1171-1252)

Salah al-Din retook Syria and recovered Jerusalem from the Crusaders. His greatest work was the remodelling of Cairo. He built the Citadel, laid out like one of the Crusader Castles in Syria. This was to dominate the city and has done since the twelfth century A.D. A new social order came into being, with a period of growth and the restoration of the old order of Sunni Muslims. Salah al-Din died in 1193. For the next twenty years, there were many battles with the Crusaders, who had realized that Egypt was the key to

Citadel of Salah al-Din in Cairo

advancement in the Middle East. The Fifth Crusade took Damietta in 1221, and the Sixth Crusade retook it but were defeated in the ensuing battle, and Saint Louis was taken prisoner at Mansura, in the Delta. He was later ransomed, only to die on the Seventh Crusade at Carthage, thus marking the end of the Crusades as far as Egypt was concerned.

The Ayyubid Dynasty collapsed with the murder of Turan Shah by Mamluk troops under their commander, Baybars, who had been brought to Egypt by the Ayyubids. The Mamluks were originally slaves, acquired from outside the Muslim area, in Europe and Central Asia. They were given a rudimentary education, converted to Islam and given military training. When this was completed, they were freed to join the State Service as Mamluks. They had become powerful enough after Turan Shah's murder to choose one of their own, the chief Mamluk, Aybak, as the next ruler; he was murdered in 1259. So here one has the astonishing result of an alien slave rising to the highest position in the state.

THE MAMLUKS (A.D. 1250-1517)

There were two dynasties of Mamluks: the Bahri Mamluks who ruled Egypt from 1250-1382, and the Circassian Mamluks, or Burgis, who ruled between 1382 1517. They took their name from the barracks where their corps were quartered. Son rarely succeeded father and changes in succession were invariably marked by bloodshed and trouble.

The first Bahri ruler was Baybars (Panther). One of his first acts was to defeat the Mongols at Ayn Jalut, near Hama in Syria. This removed a potential danger to Egypt by driving the Mongols northwards out of Syria. By so doing, he removed a possible ally of the Crusaders, as the Mongols were the only people who could have sided with the Christians against the Muslim states. So the Christian cause in hither Asia was doomed. Baybars extended his rule to Syria and by bringing one of the last of the Abbasid Princes to Cairo and establishing him as titulary Khalif, he gained control of the Sunni heart of Islam, and the support of the Sharif of Mecca. Baybars was a great traveller and his campaigns extended from Nubia in the south, to Anatolia in the north. His rule of

Egypt was enlightened, strict but just. He was greatly beloved by the common people of Cairo, who still listen in the coffee houses to tales of his prowess, such as his swimming the Nile in full armour and of his travels - one day in the Hejaz, the next in Aleppo.

The Madrasah of the Sultan Baybars I, el-Bunduqdari, is now largely ruined. It was built between 1262-63 on the site of the Eastern Palace of the Fatimids. It fell into disuse, in later Mamluk times, and in 1882 the minaret collapsed. At the time of the Napoleonic occupation, it was used as a fort (Fort Sulkowski) and later turned into a bakery, a stable and then a soap factory. The mosque, to which the madrasah was attached, had a vast colonnaded court, with monumental gates and at each corner, square towers. Baybars died in Damascus, either from poison or drinking fermented mare's milk, of which he was inordinately fond. Baybars' family failed to establish a dynasty and it was the Atabak, Qalawan who established the next line of rulers, though they were not all descended directly from him.

Qalawan was known as the al-Alfi (a thousand) because of the one thousand coins paid for him in the market. Under Qalawan, the Crusaders' position deteriorated further until they were reduced to Acre and the surrounding area. Al-Nasir Muhammad, one of Qalawan's sons, reigned at intervals till 1340 and this period marked Egypt's most prosperous time in the Middle Ages. After this, the quality of the Bahri rulers declined rapidly and there were eleven of them in the next forty years.

In 1382 the sultanate was seized by Barquq, a Circassian, stationed in the Citadel and this group, the Burgi Mamluks, ruled Egypt for the next one hundred and forty years. They produced few remarkable men, but the country on the whole prospered. Some fine buildings were constructed and trade increased. However, by 1516, the power of the Ottoman Turks was rising and Syria, a Mamluk possession, was invaded by the Turks. The last Mamluk sultan died in battle near Aleppo in August 1516. By the following year, the Turks were in Egypt. They removed the last Khalif to Istanbul to bolster their claim to the Khaliphate of Islam.

THE OTTOMAN PERIOD (A.D. 1517-1805)

The Turkish rule was disasterous for Egypt. Instead of being a sovereign state, she became one of the many vilayets of the vast Ottoman Empire, administered by a Turkish Vali and governed by foreigners from Istanbul, whose main aim was to obtain as much as possible from the provinces. Although the power of the Mamluks was broken in a political sense, they still existed as a military power and continued to recruit their number by more slaves. Having conflicting interests, the local Beys were in contention through much of the period with the governors appointed from Istanbul. Under Ottoman control, Egypt was in cultural decline and became a backwater.

THE FRENCH INTERLUDE

In 1798, Napoleon aimed to control the sea-route to India and invaded Egypt. Although the French were victorious at the Battle of the Pyramids, their fleet was defeated by Nelson and destroyed at the Battle of Abu Kir Bay. The British and Ottoman forces attempted an invasion without success, and shortly after, in 1799, Napoleon left Egypt. General Kleber was appointed governor but was assassinated and replaced by General Baron de Menou, who declared Egypt a French colony. In 1801, the British under Sir Ralph Abercromby, attacked from Abu Kir and took Alexandria, but Abercromby was killed. With Ottoman help, further advances were made as far as Cairo and the French capitulated and withdrew in 1801.

Napoleon had brought to Egypt an eminent body of French artists and scientists, who examined the country and its antiquities. They published the *Description of Egypt*, in twenty volumes, by 1828. The Rosetta Stone, discovered by the French, fell into British hands; the stone was the key to the decipherment of Egyptian hieroglyphs. The impact of French culture and technology on Egypt was shattering for a country which had been living in the Middle Ages. Having destroyed the power of the Mamluks and having ejected the Turks, they left the country in chaos.

The Ottoman Sultan, Selim III, tried to control the Mamluk Beys by having their leaders massacred at Abu Kir, but he was only partially successful. In 1803, the British evacuated Alexandria and their withdrawing forces were accompanied by Muhammad Bey, al-Alfi, one of the leading Beys who went to England to discuss means of restoring Mamluk power.

THE KHEDIVES (A.D. 1805-1922)

For the next two years Egypt was in a state of civil disorder. Muhammad Ali (c. 1769-1849), the commander of the Albanian contingent, was attacked in Cairo by his own troops and fled to the coast. He allied himself with the Mamluk Beys against the nominal Ottoman governor and was declared Pasha. He was later confirmed in this position by the Sublime Porte and was, to all intents and purposes, independent of Turkey. However, Muhammad Ali could not establish his authority or achieve the unity of Egypt until he had disposed of the Mamluk Beys, so he had most of them killed following a feast held for them in the Citadel in 1811, known as the 'Massacre of the Mamluks'. This marked the end of the Mamluks' attempts to regain power.

All public land was sequestered by the state, the government was reformed, based on European lines, departments of Education and Commerce were established and a government printing press was set up. In 1835, a Department of Public Works was formed under the direction of a Frenchman, and Egyptians were sent abroad, usually to France, to learn governmental skills they could not acquire in Egypt. However, the language of the administration remained Turkish. Muhammad Ali also reformed the army and founded the modern Egyptian navy which became one of the most powerful fleets in the Mediterranean. He encouraged agriculture and introduced the long-staple cotton from the Sudan and America in 1822, which laid the foundation of Egypt's cotton industry, now its most important export. He established a large number of monopolies on cotton, gum arabic and indigo, and the increase in Egyptian productivity and exports led to the development of Alexandria as a commercial port. The French started a shipping line between Marseilles and Alexandria in 1835, and shortly after-

His Highness Muhammad Ali, Pasha of Egypt
by Sir David Wilkie (oil on board)

41

wards the East India Company began a service of steamers between Bombay and Suez. As a result of his enlightened outlook, Muhammad Ali could be regarded as the founder of modern Egypt.

In 1813, Muhammad Ali was asked by the Sublime Porte to suppress the Wahhabi revolt in the Hejaz. The Egyptian army was first commanded by Muhammad Ali, then by his second son Tusun, who died in 1816. Muhammad Ali's eldest son, Ibrahim (1789-1848), then took control of the forces. After a difficult two year campaign during which he shared all the hardships of his troops, Ibrahim finally forced the Wahhabi leader to surrender in 1818. In 1824, Muhammad Ali was appointed Governor of the Morea by the Sultan who wanted his help against the Greeks in their War of Independence. Ibrahim was sent there in charge of the Egyptian forces and although he defeated the Greeks on land, his fleet was shattered by the Great Powers at the Battle of Navarino and he left the country in 1828. Muhammad Ali sent him to conquer Syria; he occupied Damascus, defeated the Turkish army at Homs and finally routed the Turkish Grand Vizier at Konia. Muhammad Ali stopped Ibrahim from advancing on Istanbul and toppling the Turkish Sultanate. He was appointed Pasha and briefly governor of the conquered provinces, on a yearly basis.

The Great Powers, alarmed at the possibility of Egypt overthrowing the Ottoman Empire of which she was a vassal state, forced Ibrahim's withdrawal from Anatolia and Syria, and enforced a commercial agreement upon the Ottoman Porte that destroyed Muhammad Ali's monopolies and allowed the free flow of cheap European goods, including cotton, on to the Egyptian and Syrian markets, thus destroying Egypt's incipient industries. A strong government in Egypt posed a threat to the European trade routes to the Orient, a position they were unwilling to tolerate.

In the last years of his life, Muhammad Ali was granted the hereditary title of 'Pashalik of Egypt' by the Ottoman Porte, but not independence. During Muhammad Ali's final illness, Ibrahim assumed control with Turkish assent, but he collapsed and died in November 1848. His father outlived him by nine months, but was in no state to administer the country which was ruled by his grandson Abbas after Ibrahim's death.

42

Muhammad Ali was one of the most remarkable men to have risen to power from nothing and to have a vision of what Egypt could achieve. He was stern yet generous, and as he said, "Forgiveness is the almsgiving of the victorious". Abbas, the son of Tusun, succeeded him. He abandoned some of his grandfather's reforms and was rather anti-European in attitude. Within five years he was murdered and was succeeded by his uncle, Said Pasha, another son of Muhammad Ali, who ruled between 1854 1863. He was lazy and had little idea of the value of money. It was he who granted de Lesseps, in 1856, the concession to build the Suez Canal.

ISMAIL PASHA (1863 1879)

Ismail Pasha was a son of Ibrahim Pasha and therefore another grandson of Muhammad Ali. He had been educated in France and throughout his reign he strove for autonomy from Turkey, the westernization of Egypt and the extension of Egyptian power in Africa. In spite of his European education, he was still an oriental despot and again had little idea of money. His expansionist policy ran him heavily into debt. He increased the army, claimed much of the Red Sea coastline and sent Samuel Baker, an English explorer, to annex areas in Equatorial Africa. He received the title of Khedive from the Sultan. Unfortunately, this gave him no extra revenue and by 1875 the country was bankrupt. No further loans could be raised on the international market, so Ismail was forced, in 1875, to sell his Canal shares to Britain for some four million pounds. Egyptian financial affairs were put under British and French supervision. This did not work and Ismail dismissed his ministers. Thereupon the Turkish Sultan, under pressure from Britain and France, forced Ismail's resignation and appointed his son, Muhammad Tewfik, Pasha in 1879.

THE BRITISH OCCUPATION AND THE RISE OF NATIONAL-ISM

In 1872 the rise of nationalism began, fuelled by a pan-Islamic agitator, al-Sayyid Jamal al-Din al Afgani. An Afghan by birth, he came to Egypt and spoke at large meetings in Cairo calling for

Muslims to resist westernization. This alarmed the government and al-Afgani was expelled from Egypt. He went to Paris and with an Egyptian, set up a journal criticizing British policy in Muslim countries. Many people in France and elsewhere felt that Egyptians were being unjustly punished for Ismail's personal mistakes. Foreign control of Egypt's finances caused a lot of resentment, particularly among army officers. There was also resentment amongst Arabic-speaking junior officers of the Turkish-speaking elite, in the higher ranks of the army. Arabi, a colonel of peasant origin, became the symbol for the protest against foreign control, Turkish or European, and he was the figurehead of the revolt which erupted in 1882. Muhammad Tewfik was unable to control the movement, and a nationalist ministry, which included Arabi, was forced on the Khedive in 1882.

The danger of a national uprising brought both British and French fleets to Alexandria, where following a massacre, they bombarded the city in July. The British Government, wishing to suppress the growing revolt, asked the French and Italians to help. When they declined, the British went ahead alone. Sir Garnet Wolseley led an expeditionary force from Ismailia in the Canal zone to Tel-el-Kebir, where Arabi's main army was defeated in September 1882. He surrendered soon afterwards and was banished, along with other leaders of the revolt. This led to the British occupation of Egypt.

The British Government sent Lord Dufferin, British Ambassador to the Ottoman Empire, to Egypt to report on what needed to be done and in March, 1883, he published his report laying down the main principles on which Egypt should be governed. Sir Evelyn Baring was appointed British Agent and Consul General and to him fell the task of implementing Dufferin's report. The old Egyptian army was disbanded and a new force, under Sir Evelyn Wood, the new Sirdar, was set up with both British and Egyptian officers, numbering about four thousand men. It was smaller and more efficient than the old army and conditions of service were improved. There was also a British army of occupation which fluctuated greatly in numbers, but rarely exceeded fourteen thousand men.

An organic law, drafted under Lord Dufferin's supervision, dealt with the government of Egypt. Consultative councils were set up in each province, varying in number from three to eight according to the size and population of the province. A legislative assembly of thirty members was set up for the whole country, partly appointed and partly elected. There was also a legislative assembly consisting of the thirty council members and forty-six elected members, as well as the ministers of the different departments.

At the same time, the British Government managed in 1883 to obtain greater representation on the board of management of the Suez Canal, although the majority still remained French. Both Britain and France supported the demand that the first call on Egyptian resources should be the repayment of creditors, but Baring's difficulties were compounded by the lack of consistent guidance from the home government, which was anxious to withdraw the British forces as soon as possible. The Mahadist revolt in the Sudan upset all the financial arrangements in the country; the Egyptian garrisons in the Sudan were withdrawn and the whole of the Sudan south of Wadi Halfa was evacuated and Nubia was made a military zone.

In 1885, the London Convention was signed reducing the interest on the national debt and enabling the Egyptian Government to raise an international loan. In 1890, a new municipal council was established in the capital, with twenty-eight members, half elected and half government appointees, led by the city governor. Baring devoted himself to preventing Egypt from becoming bankrupt again and under his guiding hand many reforms took place. He was undoubtedly the architect of the new Egypt that slowly emerged. Forced labour was abolished, long-term hydrographic studies were undertaken and barrages were built in an attempt to control the Nile. He improved irrigation and got the Delta barrages working, a scheme started by Muhammad Ali. The building of the first Aswan High Dam between 1898 and 1902 increased crop yields in Upper Egypt. Education, public health and the law were also reformed. Modernization of the larger towns was started and better roads and the sewerage system were begun in Cairo. In 1892, Baring was elevated to the peerage as Baron Cromer.

ABBAS II (1892-1914)

The Khedive Muhammad Tewfik died in January 1892 and was succeeded by his son Abbas Hilmi, a young man anxious to be rid of British control. He dismissed the Prime Minister, Mustafa Fahmi Pasha, whom he considered to be too pro-British. He encouraged anti-British attitudes and negotiated with the nationalist faction. For a time, he appointed Husain Fakri Pasha, a nationalist sympathizer, to be Prime Minister. However, in 1895 Mustafa Fahmi Pasha regained his position and continued in office for a considerable period.

The nationalist movement that had been quiescent for about ten years after 1882 now revived and Mustafa Kamil, a young French educated lawyer, founded the second nationalist party, advocating independence through legal means. In 1899, a periodical was started to voice the party's views and had a wide circulation. Also in 1899, Arabi Pasha returned from exile in Ceylon. His return did not cause much of a stir and he found himself forgotten by the younger nationalists. The cause for independence was popular among the educated Copts, but they were only interested in Egyptian nationalism and not in pan-Arabism.

THE PROBLEM OF THE SUDAN

The rise to power of the Mahdi and the withdrawal of the Egyptian forces from the Sudan in 1884-5 caused international repercussions. The French claimed the latter was a lapse of Egyptian sovereignty, which Britain disputed. The European scramble for Africa resulted in the Sudan being surrounded by territories occupied by the French, Belgians, Italians and British, with Ethiopia under the strong emperor, Melik II. And they all had their eyes on the Sudan.

General Gordon had been sent to the Sudan as Governor General so as to pacify it and to withdraw the Egyptian garrisons and personnel. His instructions were ambiguous and before the withdrawal was completed the Mahdi rejected his peace offers which made further action impossible. Gordon was besieged in Khartoum by the Mahdi. There were repeated attacks and a growing shortage of food. The British Government under Gladstone, procrastinated about sending a relief force and after nine months Khartoum fell and Gordon was murdered by the Mahdi's troops, in January 1885. The whole thing was unnecessary and Gordon was sacrificed to the whims of a British Liberal Government.

For thirteen years the Mahdi was in control. The slave trade revived and he posed a serious threat to the stability of Egypt. This, together with the indignation over Gordon's death, led to General Kitchener, Sirdar of the Egyptian army, being sent to the Sudan. The French had occupied Fashoda, on the White Nile, and a Franco-Ethiopian expedition marched westwards towards the town in an attempt to establish a base there and lay claim to the Sudan. Kitchener led an escort to Fashoda and asked the French to withdraw from the Khedive's dominions. The whole incident nearly led to war between Britain and France. Meanwhile, Kitchener destroyed the Mahdi's forces at the Battle of Omdurman in September 1898.

The future of the Sudan and matters between Britain and France were settled in the Convention signed by Britain and Egypt in January 1899, and two months later, France abandoned all claims to the Nile Valley. Power in the Sudan was invested in a governor general appointed by the Khedive on the recommendation of Britain, and the Northern boundary was defined. Turkey protested that the agreement transgressed the rights of the Sultan as the sovereign power, but in vain.

The long period of tension between Britain and France ended in a declaration signed in April 1904, by which Britain recognized the claim of France to Morocco and France recognized Britain's claim to Egypt. Britain then turned her attention to the boundaries of Sinai in order to protect her interests in the Suez Canal.

SINAI

The borders of Sinai had never been properly fixed. From 1841-92 Sinai was not administrated by anyone. Theoretically it was part of the Ottoman Empire, which allowed Egypt to keep a police post in the south to protect the pilgrims going to and from Mecca. Under Tewfik, it was agreed that South Sinai should be administ-

Lord Kitchener of Khartoum, GCB, KCMG

ered by Egypt. But when the pilgrims went by sea rather than by land, the Ottoman Government, in 1906, wished to resume possession of the area and in February 1906, a Turkish patrol occupied Tabah, on the west coast of the Gulf of Aqaba. The Khedive Abbas refused to make a claim on Egypt's behalf, so Lord Cromer appealed to Constantinople. The Sultan gave way and the Turkish patrol was withdrawn. In an agreement signed by the Porte and the Egyptian Government in October 1906, Ottoman sovereignty over the disputed area was recognized; the administration was invested with Egypt and the boundary with Palestine was fixed in a straight line, running from Rafah to Aqaba.

EGYPT (1907-1914)

In April 1907, the long domination of Egyptian affairs by Lord Cromer ended with his resignation. He was replaced by Sir J. Eldon Gorst, who had a more liberal outlook. Cromer had been quite unable to understand the move towards nationalism and independence. Gorst died in July 1911, having failed in most of his schemes for a moderate constitutional and liberal advance.

In September 1911, Herbert Kitchener was appointed to succeed him as British Agent and Consul General. Between 1907 and 1914, the first peasants' co-operatives were established and Kitchener continued to introduce reforms. He was especially interested in the welfare of the peasants. In 1912, a measure known as the Five Feddans Law was passed; this exempted small holdings from seizure for debt. This aimed, like the later law introduced by Nasser, to give the peasants a small holding of five to six feddans, a water buffalo and a water-wheel. Another important measure was the law of July 1913, which reduced the national assembly to one of sixty-six members elected by indirect vote and seventeen appointed by the government to represent minorities.

The Khedive Abbas interferred less with the government after the appointment of the new assembly, but he remained strongly against the British occupation and did not have good relations with Kitchener. The latter was in England, on leave, at the outbreak of the First World War and was asked by the government to remain in England to become Secretary of State for War. As a result, he never returned to Egypt. At the beginning of the war, Abbas was in Constantinople. He had already made known his support for Turkey in the war and was therefore forbidden to return to Egypt. The Egyptian Government was forced to support the British side, the legislative assembly was suspended indefinitely and on 2nd November 1914, martial law was introduced, remaining in force until the end of the war. Egypt's position vis-à-vis Turkey was impossible and as a result, on 18th December 1914, a British Protectorate was declared over the country.

THE BRITISH PROTECTORATE

Following the declaration of the Protectorate, the Khedive Abbas was deposed in his absence and his uncle, Hasain Kamil, was declared ruler with the title of Sultan. With the departure of Kitchener, a new British Agent and Consul General was appointed, Sir Henry McMahon. Some British officials were withdrawn for the war effort, but many remained and the bulk of Egyptians in the Civil Service regarded them as a bar to promotion. The students also disliked the British presence and as the number of universities increased so did the anti-British feeling. Egypt prospered materially during the war, which was not popular as there was a feeling that Egypt had been drawn into a conflict that did not concern her. By the end of 1916, Sir Reginald Wingate, who had served as Sirdar and Governor General of the Sudan since 1899, replaced McMahon as British High Commissioner. Husain Kamil's health declined and the question arose as to who would be his successor. His son, Prince Kamil el-Din, refused the position, which then went to Prince Fuad, the sixth and youngest son of Ismail, who had been educated in Italy. It was just as well arrangements had been made as Sultan Husain died in October 1917. At the close of the war, Egypt thought it had a right to independence and to be represented at the Peace Conference. The British Foreign Office rejected this claim and also the suggestion that Egyptian ministers should go to London to argue their case, even though the idea had been supported by Wingate. Zaghul, head of the Wafd (Nationalists), was refused permission to go to London and plead for independence. Martial law was again invoked, and Zaghul and three of his most important supporters were arrested in March 1919 and exiled to Malta.

50

Disturbances and revolts broke out in various Egyptian cities. Railway and telephone lines were cut and British subjects murdered. Every class of the population was involved, including the fellahin, who in the past had benefited most from British rule. Field Marshal Lord Allenby, who had replaced Wingate, put down what amounted to a rebellion and once order had been restored, he initiated a policy of reconciliation. As a result, the British Government sent Lord Milner to Egypt to assess the situation. Informal discussions were held and Zaghul and his associates were permitted to leave Malta and go to the Peace Conference, although they did not receive a hearing. It became apparent to Milner that the majority of Egyptians were thoroughly dissatisfied with the existing state of affairs and he presented the British Government with a very fair assessment of the situation. Consequently, Zaghul was invited to London to state his case, and the Milner-Zaghul Agreement was drafted. This allowed for Egypt's independence in return for a treaty of alliance, under which Egypt contracted certain obligations. These the Egyptians could not agree to and Britain made a unilateral declaration on 28th February 1922, declaring Egypt a sovereign state but keeping the Suez Canal, Foreign Relations, the Nile Waters and the Sudan under British control. Despite Fuad assuming the title of king and declaring Egypt independent in March 1922, the result was only partial independence, which solved nothing.

The British Government refused to negotiate on the question of the Sudan. Zaghul went to England for talks but the points of view of the two governments were irreconcilable and on his return, Zaghul surrounded himself with nationalist ministers, instead of the moderate ones. On 19th November 1924, Sir Lee Stack, the Sirdar and Governor General of the Sudan, was shot and killed while driving through the streets of Cairo. His assassination roused a storm of protest from the British people. Allenby put forward terms that amounted to an ultimatum. His Majesty's Government demanded that the Egyptian Government should apologize for the crime, enquire as to who had committed it, suppress and forbid all political demonstrations, pay a fine amounting to five hundred thousand pounds and withdraw all Egyptian officers and men from the Sudan. Other measures included increasing the amount of irrigation in the Sudan, thus drawing off the waters of the Nile from Egypt. The Egyptian Government refused the measures connected with the Sudan but they did withdraw their forces and as a result, the Sudanese Defence Force was formed, owing allegiance only to the Sudanese Government.

NEGOTIATIONS (1924-1936)

The question of complete independence, the presence of British troops in Egypt, the Suez Canal and the Sudan, dominated Egyptian domestic politics during the 1920s and 1930s. The situation was unstable, with the nationalists pulling one way, the palace under King Fuad, another, with the British having the final word. Although the Wafd was not acceptable to either the king or the British, they were the only party strong enough to effect a settlement with the British Government. Zaghul was succeeded by Mustapha al-Nahas Pasha and negotiations ground on under Lord Lloyd, who had succeeded Allenby in 1925. Matters were temporarily settled in 1935 by the restoration of the 1923 constitution. King Fuad died in April 1936, and was succeeded by his young son, Faruq, who got on no better with Nahas than his father had with Zaghul. Foreign affairs dominated domestic matters as Egypt feared she would be drawn into the Italian-Abyssinian war. Eventually after years of trouble, the Anglo-Egyptian Treaty was signed in London in April 1936, and ratified in Cairo in December 1936. It was to run for twenty years with a possible revision after ten years. Article seven listed the aid which Egypt would give, in time of war, to Britain. It was unfortunate that this clause had to be invoked so soon, with the outbreak of the Second World War.

Egypt suffered during the war from shortages like the rest of the world and cotton exports were disrupted. There was a direct threat of a German-Italian invasion which receded after the Battle of el-Alamein in 1942. Once the danger of invasion was over, demands for complete independence increased and when the war was over the Wafd Press agitated for the revision of the treaty, the evacuation of British troops and union with the Sudan. This, the British Government could not accept as they wished the Sudan to be independent. In November 1945 and February 1946, there were riots in Cairo and Alexandria, especially among the students, and in March, further trouble was caused by the Muslim Brother-hood (Ikhwan al-Muslimin). British troops were withdrawn from Cairo, Alexandria and the Canal Zone in 1947 and in 1948 Britain granted self-government to the Sudan, against the wishes of Egypt, who took the case to the United Nations, with the backing of the Arab League, but with no success.

The vast influx of Jews into Palestine after the war, caused the Arabs there to rebel, which made Britain's position in Palestine untenable. She resigned her mandate there in May 1948 to the United Nations and Israel unilaterally declared itself an independ-ent state. Egypt, together with members of the Arab League, attacked Israel with partial success. The major powers recognized the State of Israel, to the disgust of Egypt and the Arab League, and a ceasefire was engineered by the United Nations, who gave Gaza to Egypt and Beersheba to Israel as part of the armistice.

Nahas was dismissed, and in July 1952, there was a *coup d'état* led by General Muhammad Naguib. King Faruq was forced to abdicate by the revolutionary council. Egypt was then declared a republic on 18th June 1953.

THE REPUBLIC OF EGYPT

Naguib was not in power for long. By June 1956, the last British soldiers had left the Canal Zone, and three days later, General abd al-Nasser, head of the revolutionary council, was declared Presid-ent. He assumed supreme power after a referendum. This was the first time since the Thirtieth Dynasty in the fourth century B.C. that Egypt was ruled by an Egyptian.

One of Nasser's first actions was the re-allocation of land. No one was to hold more than one hundred feddans of land; the ultimate aim being that all peasants should own their own land. The resulting break-up of the big estates meant the destruction of the cattle herds as the poorer farmers could not afford to support them on their small holdings. This resulted in large numbers of cattle being slaughtered and meat rationing had to be introduced. In 1952, because of the growth of population, Egypt was no longer self-supporting. In an attempt to control the waters of the Nile and increase perennial irrigation, Nasser decided to build a further high dam enclosing the area of the river between Wadi Halfa and Aswan, thus virtually destroying Nubia.

The concession to build the dam was first offered to Great Britain and the United States, but their experts did not consider it a viable proposition. Nasser, therefore, nationalized the Suez Canal to pay for the dam. As a result, Israel, with British and French support, launched an attack on Egypt on 29th October 1956. Under pressure from America and having alienated Egypt, Britain and France withdrew and a United Nations peace-keeping force was installed. The Canal, which had been blocked by Egypt, remained closed until April 1957. In 1958, the USSR granted Egypt a long-term loan to finance the building of the new high dam and it was built by Russian engineers.

In January 1958, a union with Syria was announced, to be known as the United Arab Republic and with Nasser as president. Unfortunately, the Egyptians treated Syria more as a conquered country than as an ally and sent petty officials to administer every district. The Syrians, for their part, did not regard the Egyptians as true Arabs. As a result, the union was a disaster and was dissolved in 1961. The following year, Nasser involved Egypt in a war with the Yemen, which led to the overthrow of the Imam. The war was an economic drain on Egypt that she could ill afford and caused the loss of a large number of Egyptian soldiers.

As the Americans did not like the policies Egypt was following, they terminated the economic aid they had been giving to her, much of which had not been received by those to whom it was intended. This caused Nasser to turn to the USSR for help. Egypt's economy was in ruins: there was a shortage of commodities, there was no money to pay for the High Dam, so she had to pay in kind, which meant the sugar, rice and cotton crops going to Russia. To add to her economic difficulties, there was another clash with Israel over the rights of navigation in the Straits of Tiran. Between the 5th and 8th June 1967, the Israelies occupied Sinai and were soon entrenched on the east bank of the Suez Canal. The Egyptians had their armoured columns destroyed. They knew nothing about modern desert warfare and were hopelessly outclassed. Nasser resigned, but the people of Egypt turned out in their thousands to support him and refused to accept his resignation. He had extra-

President Nasser and the British Foreign Secretary, Selwyn Lloyd

ordinary charisma, which appeals to the masses. After the disastrous Six Day War, Egyptians took their military training more seriously. They found the equipment they had received from the Russians was in many ways deficient, so Nasser approached the United States for supplies, to which they responded.

In September 1970, the Arab League held a conference in Cairo, which then became its headquarters. The day after the conference, Nasser died and the city saw scenes of unprecedented mourning at his funeral. He was succeeded by Anwar el-Sadat, who had also been a member of the revolutionary council, and had been at the military college with Nasser. He was elected president in October 1971. On the completion of the High Dam, the Russians wished to establish an airforce base near Aswan. This the Egyptians thought undesirable and Sadat expelled the Soviet presence in Egypt on the grounds that it was damaging the independence and stability of the state.

On 6th October 1972, Sadat after a carefully planned campaign invaded Sinai on Yom al-Kippur, the holiest day of the Jewish calendar, and caught the Israelis unprepared. The October War, as it was called, was an unprecedented success and enabled the Egyptians to negotiate with the Israelis from a position of strength. With the assistance of the United States, the Camp David Agreement was made as a preliminary to peace with Israel. This led to the withdrawal of the Israelis from Sinai and its return to Egypt. For this agreement, Egypt lost the support of the other Arab states and the headquarters of the Arab League was moved from Cairo. Except for Saudi Arabia and Jordan, most Arab States broke off diplomatic relations with Egypt and the League now meets elsewhere. It was not until 1989 at the Casablanca Conference that Egypt was restored as a member. President Sadat was assassinated on the 6th October 1981, while attending an army parade. His assassins were religious dissidents, some of them army personnel. He was succeeded by the vice-president, Husni Mubarak.

Mubarak has continued Sadat's policies and appears more popular than Sadat, who had a better international image than internal reputation. Egypt faces many problems. The High Dam has not proved the panacea it was hoped, nor has it fulfilled its quota of electricity supplies for the country. The lack of rain in

Ethiopia and Central Africa has led to Lake Nasser not being filled to capacity, despite the rain in the Sudan in 1988. This has affected irrigation and the planting of the cotton and rice crops. The population is increasing rapidly and is now about fifty million, with over ten million in Greater Cairo. Egypt is an African country, her economy inseparable from the Nile, and therefore unpredictable.

RELIGION

Egypt has known many religions. In ancient times, the Egyptians were polytheists and according to Greek sources, the most religious people in the ancient world. They equated the rising of the sun with life and the setting of the sun with death. The south, where the Nile was thought to rise in a cavern from the primeval waters, was the region of life, while the north, where the Nile flowed into the sea, was the region of death. The west belonged to Osiris and the stars they identified with the souls of the dead. At the beginning, the world was thought of as rising from the watery waste of Nun, Chaos, similar to the islands they saw when the inundation of the Nile subsided. These primeval mounds were very important in Egyptian religion; they were associated with Osiris, the god of the dead, and the sanctuary of every temple in Egypt was supposed to have been built over one of them. At the end of the world, gods, men, everything would be returned to the watery waste of Nun.

From early times, Egyptians worshipped the two great mother goddesses, who were the protectors of the kings of Egypt. They were Nekhbet, the vulture goddess of Upper Egypt, and Wadjet, the cobra goddess of Lower Egypt. However, each of the main cities had their own deities. These were mainly triads: a god, a goddess, and their son. There were exceptions to this; Khnum, the ram god of the First Cataract, who formed mankind on his potter's wheel and his two wives, Satet and Anuket, who were the goddesses of the inundation. Hermopolis had an ogdoad consisting of Nu and Nunet, Amun and Amunet, Heh and Hehet and Ke and Kehet, who represented the gods of chaos and disorder.

Heliopolis (ancient On) had one of the most important groups of gods. The oldest god, according to the Pyramid Texts, was Father Atum who was "before the earth, the sky, men or gods had come into being". He was thought to have created the world from the watery waste of Nun. Atum was the creator of all things; he made Shu, the god of wind and Tefnut, the goddess of moisture. He also created Geb, the earth god and Nut, the sky goddess whose children were Osiris, Isis, Seth, Nephthys and Horus the Elder. It was from Heliopolis that most of the Egyptian religious rituals derived and it was the Heliopolitan order that was later followed in most of the temples throughout the land.

Osiris, Anubis and Horus the Elder from the tomb of Horemheb in the Valley of the Kings, Thebes

The repetitive, divine services saved Egypt from chaos and gave her stability. The Egyptians' fear of chaos and their desire for an orderly way of life led to the conception of the goddess Ma'at, who stood for law, order, truth and justice and it was this tenet that governed their way of life. The king was regarded as the intermediary between the gods and man and as such had a semi-divine status. He was titular head of every priesthood and as such was shown on temple walls making offerings to the gods. These offerings were a two way thing: in return for incense, food and drink the king was promised long life and a successful reign.

Memphis was another great centre of religious learning; here the triad was Ptah, Sekhmet and Nefertum. Ptah was the protector of craftsmen; he had various forms and according to the Shabaka stone, which dates from the Twenty-fifth Dynasty and is a copy of an older text, he created the world by the Word of God, rather than by a physical creation, thus pre-dating the New Testament by many centuries. His wife, Sekhmet, was the daughter of Re and a sun-goddess representing the fierce rays of the sun. Nefertum, their son, was shown as a young god seated on a lotus flower. Later, he was partially replaced by Imhotep, the deified chief of works of Djoser, king of the Third Dynasty, who designed the Step Pyramid. Imhotep was associated in the Egyptian mind with the art of healing.

Another creation legend is the one according to Neith, found inscribed in the temple of Esna. Neith was the patron goddess of Lower Egypt. She created Egypt "in gladness" and Re, the sun god, whom she made the chief deity. Mankind was created from the tears of his eyes. At the same time, Apopi, a giant serpent, appeared, who would lead the revolt against Re, as there must always be a balance between good and evil in Egypt.

As well as the very sophisticated idea of the creation of the world by the Word of God, the Egyptians had another remarkable conception, that of the resurrection. This was a belief universally held throughout Egypt, following the worship of Osiris, who was murdered but rose to live again. Thus with his resurrection, the promise of life after death was given to all mankind. His cult centre was at Abydos, which consequently became one of the main places of pilgrimage. Osiris and Re contended for the position of supreme god in Egypt. Re however was more of a royal deity whereas Osiris became the deity of the people.

The murder of Osiris by his brother Seth and the battles Horus fought to avenge the death of his father are the archetypal struggles of good against evil and as such appealed to everyone. It was in fact the soul of the land of Egypt for which they were struggling and the balance of the Two Lands was Memphis. The battle became the subject of religious plays and one of the most important of the Egyptian legends.

There were two types of temple in the Old Kingdom: the state temple where the state gods were worshipped and the mortuary temple where the dead kings were worshipped. From the New Kingdom onwards, the temples had the same layout, with a few exceptions, such as the Seti I temple at Abydos.

Mortuary Temple of Hatshepsut at Deir el-Bahari

The problem as to whether the Egyptians believed in one god or many is difficult to resolve. Towards the end of Ancient Egyptian history, there was a tendency to amalgamate the deities, a concept probably more Hellenistic than Egyptian.

In the First Century A.D., Egypt was converted to Christianity, traditionally by St. Mark. This did not happen overnight and it took a long time for the old beliefs to be swept away. The last text to the old gods is at Philae dated A.D. 473. Christianity was first established in Alexandria. We know little about the foundation of the Alexandrine church and there is scant information until the episcopate of Demetrius (A.D. 189-231) when the church appeared as a flourishing community. After this, it was severely persecuted, first under the Roman Emperor Decius (A.D. 249-251) and again under the Emperor Diocletian (A.D. 284-305). So severe was the second persecution that the Copts (Egyptian Christians) call their calendar the Martyr's Calendar, which dates from Diocletian's accession.

The decrees of the Council of Chalcedon in 451, were not accepted by the majority of Egypt's Christians and they formed a separate schismatic body, the Monophistic Church, known as the Coptic Church, separate from the Greek Orthodox Church, which was the church of the Byzantine Empire. The history of the period between 451-641 when the Arabs invaded is very confused. It is marked by fruitless attempts of Byzantine emperors to impose their will on Egypt and it was during these two centuries that Egyptian Christians assumed their distinctive character and their unbending fanaticism.

The connection with Constantinople was severed with the conquest of Egypt by the Muslims, which began in A.D. 639. At first, the Copts were treated kindly but later their taxes were increased and they suffered severe persecution, so that the majority became converts to Islam.

It was the Copts who were the founders of monasticism, which was Egypt's most lasting contribution to Christianity, though not its only one. They played a vital role in the turbulent affairs of the early Christian Church. One of the reasons for this was the importance of the Catechetical School in Alexandria, founded in A.D. 180. This became an early centre of Christian scholarship, headed by men like Clement and Origen.

It is difficult to know how many Copts there are in Egypt today; the official census gives between seven to ten percent, but the Copts claim that they are a good deal more numerous. They are to be found mainly in Upper Egypt and Alexandria. Their head is the Coptic Patriarch, whose seat is now at St. Marks in Cairo, having moved from Alexandria in the eleventh century. There are twenty-five other bishops and metropolitans in Egypt.

The majority of Egyptians today are Muslims of the Sunni, or Orthodox persuasion. Islam means submission to God (Allah) and is believed to be the only true religion, professed by prophets from Adam onwards, terminating with the final revelation by Muhammad whose sayings were collected in the Quran. The acts enjoined on Muslims are five in number, sometimes called the Pillars of Faith. They are the pronouncing of the formula of faith that there is only One God and Muhammad is the messenger of God; prayer five times a day - at dawn, noon, mid-afternoon, sunset and midnight; the payment of alms of up to one third of one's income to the poor; fasting for the month of Ramadan and the pilgrimage to Mecca.

In the country, the two faiths, Muslim and Christian, live next door to each other; many villages have mosques and churches side by side. Even their graveyards are similar, being influenced more by ancient customs than by modern. Muslims have a series of rites and festivals of which the pilgrimage to Mecca is the most important. All are enjoined to make this but of course many cannot afford to. All, however, can fast through the month of Ramadan and at the end of this is the Id al-Sagir or Little Festival, or the Id al-Fatr, the Breaking of the Fast, when everyone dresses up in their best clothes, with those who can buying new ones, and special foods and sweetmeats are eaten. This combined with a Festival of the Dead, when families visit the graves of their relatives, palm branches are laid on the graves and food is distributed to the poor at the cemeteries. Sometimes tents are pitched and families stay overnight at the graveside. The great Muslim cemeteries in Cairo at this time are a scene of tremendous activity, with many families visiting and holding parties in the cemeteries. Another important festival is that of *Nebi Musa*, the Feast of Moses, which extends over Easter, if one follows the Greek Orthodox calendar.

Mosque of Abu el-Haggag, Luxor

Both Muslims and Christians have many celebrations called *Mawalid*, in memory of a saint. They also celebrate the *Mulid al-Nebi*, the birthday of the Prophet Muhammad. The most important Coptic festival, besides Christmas and Easter, which they keep according to their calendar, is *Shems al Nasim* or Smelling the Air, the spring festival in April which lasts three or four days and replaces the Ancient Egyptian New Year festival. Muslims partake of Christian Mawalid and vice versa, and saints like Sitta Nefisa and Sayyida Zainab play a considerable part in Cairene devotional life.

There are still small minorities of Greek Orthodox Christians, Roman Catholics and a small number of Jews, mainly in Cairo.

DAILY LIFE

Egypt is primarily a rural country and the bulk of the population are peasants. It is difficult to estimate the population of Ancient Egypt as no census was kept. In 1952, on the eve of the agrarian reform, the pressure on land greatly increased. The density of people had risen to six hundred and fifty per square kilometre and Egypt was well on the way to becoming one of the densest populated countries in the world, resembling China and India. The estimated population in 1985/6 was 48.85 million, and in greater Cairo over 10 million.

LAW - In Ancient Egypt, there were two viziers, one for the south and one for the north, who administered justice on behalf of the king. They officiated in open courts, assisted by a band of officers. Only the king had the right to impose the death penalty. An excellent account of the appointment and duties of a vizier is set out in the tomb chapel of Rekhmire, one of Tuthmosis III's viziers in the Eighteenth Dynasty, on the West Bank of Thebes. Many civil case histories have survived, some of which show the important position women had in Ancient Egypt. They held land and, in many cases, inheritance passed through the female line, a position that lasted until the Ptolemaic Period. Despite this wealth of material, no written code of law has yet been found. Policing the state in the Old Kingdom was done by local appointees; in the New Kingdom, they were replaced by Nubians, known as the Medjay.

SCRIBES - In Ancient Egypt, scribes were held in great esteem; they drew up wills and other documents for the illiterate, carried on correspondence with high officials and were in charge of the distribution of rations, tools and other requirements in the workmen's villages. One of their most important jobs was the annual cattle count for the king and in the Eighteenth Dynasty, they kept the annals of the king's wars. Each temple had a library with a scribe in charge. The temple accounts were kept here and lists of the festivals on rolls of papyrus.

THE TOMB BUILDERS - The men who worked on the construction of the tombs of the kings and queens were all freemen of the Land of Egypt. An immense amount of written evidence on ostraca, scraps of stone and papyri has come from one of the workmen's villages, Deir el-Medina. It is known that they worked shifts, each having a foreman in charge and a scribe attached to each gang. They worked a nine day week, the tenth being a day of rest. Craftsmen such as carpenters, draughtsmen, painters, artists and stonemasons also worked in the gangs. The state provided slaves for the workmen's families on certain days each month, to do the housework and make the bread. In addition, serfs were employed to fetch water from the river to fill the village cistern, to fish and get vegetables and game; they also had to collect the grain from the government stores, which was the workmen's chief ration. The highly decorated tombs of the workmen can be seen nearby.

VILLAGES - The fellahin live in villages built of mud-brick. The same method of building has been used since the beginning of early history. The villages were rebuilt in the same place, century after century, so the ground gradually rose until they were situated on mounds of considerable height, known as *koms* or *tells*, which meant artificial mounds. These mounds became islands during the annual inundation, and tracks between the villages ran on raised areas called *bunds*. The houses, we see today, have changed little over the centuries. They may be of one or two storeys, mud-plastered or white-washed with a staircase on the outside leading to a flat roof, where the owners sleep in the summer. Domed, mud granaries are built on the roof to store the grain and surplus crops and materials are stored up there. Either on the roof or in the upper walls are *malakef*, ventilators, facing north to allow the prevailing wind to cool the house. Houses are set round a courtyard which contains a domed baking oven. In the homes of wealthier Egyptians, courtyards may have a small garden with vines and fruit trees. Gardens have always been very important and people living in high-rise blocks of flats in the cities today often buy a field in the country where they can plant flowers, trees and vegetables. Outside the house there is often to be found a mud-brick bench, called a *mastaba*, where people sit and talk. The word *mastaba* was adopted by Mariette, the first Director of Antiquities, to describe the flat-topped tombs of early dynasties because of their similarity in shape to the benches. Some of the houses have gaily-painted scenes of boats, trains, planes, camels and mosques, which is an indication that the owner has made the *Hajj* or pilgrimage to Mecca.

House of a villager who has made the pilgrimage to Mecca in Gourna, W. Bank

There is, on the whole, little furniture in a poor village house, the pride of place usually going to a brass bed in the middle of the room. Clothes are kept in chests; little use being made of brick furniture, as there is further east, in Syria. If there is no bed, a mud shelf is used and the bedding rolled up during the day. The inside walls are often decorated with pictures of Alpine snow scenes. Shoes are usually taken off when entering the house to avoid spreading mud about the floor, although the rooms are frequently used as nesting places for the family birds, chickens and ducks. Dogs are not allowed indoors, as they are considered unclean. About twenty years ago, it became fashionable to build village houses in baked brick, as they had been during the Roman Period. This was not popular with the government as it meant stripping off large areas of top soil. It was prohibited in 1987, but the practice still goes on. Officially, houses can only be built of breeze-blocks, cement or pressed sugar cane. The latter warps badly and the cement is of a very poor quality because of the amount of salt in the sand.

One of the largest houses in the village is that of the *Omdah* or headman. He is usually one of the richest men in the village and is appointed, but not paid, by the government. It is his duty to see that order is maintained, and to entertain visiting notables and government officials. He also has to appoint the night-watchmen, that is any able-bodied men of good repute who possess a rifle, and to generally see that things in his area are running smoothly. His house is arranged on a slightly different plan. There always has to be a large room for entertaining, in which high-backed chairs, if possible reproduction gilt French Empire, are placed round the walls. The *Omdah* sits in the middle of one side. When he entertains, guests are offered mint tea or coffee and if more solid refreshment, such as a meat dish or rice pudding, is given, tables are brought in and placed before the guests.

The way of life has also altered little over the centuries. The main change of the last few years has been the piping of sweet water to the majority of villages, which the women fetch from a stand-pipe. Otherwise they get their water from a well or the river, and carry it in a two-handled jar, called a *bolas*, placed on a small pad of material balanced on their heads. Water is stored at the house in a porous jar, called a *zir*, which has a pointed base and is usually buried half-way up to keep it cool. The villages are, on the whole, self-contained, usually having one or two sewing machines, a tailor and a seamstress, who makes all the clothes. The long robe or *gallabiah*, worn by the men, is of ancient origin; Petrie found representations of them in a Sixth Dynasty tomb at Deshasheh. The veils worn by women are also very old. Material for the clothes is bought in the nearest town or from travelling salesmen. The village is visited weekly by a series of services, in carts pulled by donkeys. These supply tinware for cooking, washing and storage, and groceries of various kinds. A paraffin tanker comes with fuel for the primus stove, storm lanterns and pressure lamps, where there is no electricity.

A shop in Aswan selling spices and baskets

A village of any size now has a clinic; they are very basic, but will have a doctor with all the latest qualifications, as by law it is required that every medical graduate serves some years in a village. Many of the villagers, especially the women, have never left their village, even to go to the nearest town. The men, because of compulsory military service, are more likely to have travelled a little.

Boy and girl weaving a carpet near Giza

It is still customary, though not universal, to marry one's first cousin, unless active dislike is felt for the person concerned. This keeps property in the family. Although up to four wives are allowed by Islamic law, most peasants only have one wife; if she falls ill or dies, a second wife is occasionally taken. It is the bride price that limits the number of wives and also the problems caused by several wives in a small home. Some men, on obtaining unexpected riches, go out and buy a second wife, seldom from the home village. This behaviour is not well thought of, and may lead to a family being ostracized for a time.

Like the Ancient Egyptians, many country people still think that they have a double. This they call the *Karim*, as opposed to the ancient name *ka*. It has become more of a malicious spirit than a double and it is this that causes you to miss a bus, put on the wrong shoe or sandal, and causes you to do the wrong thing in an emergency. It is not really dangerous, except to young children. After the age of seven, they consider the danger becomes minimal.

WORK - Most villagers own a small amount of land which enables them to grow the necessary vegetables and some maize for feeding their animals. Most keep a donkey, a few hens, ducks and sometimes turkeys. The water-buffalo is their most prized animal. Pigeons are kept in large dove-cotes which look like crenellated forts and are a striking architectural feature on the outskirts of many villages. Egyptian hens will not sit on their eggs, probably due to inbreeding, so the eggs have to be collected and put in communal incubators, where they are turned by an attendant until hatched. This skill has been going on for thousands of years. The incubation houses are painted with pictures of cocks and hens on the outside walls.

The men work in the fields from sunrise to midday, when a meal is brought to them by the women. This is usually bread, onions, tomatoes, perhaps a cucumber or two and tea. Sweet tea is drunk in large quantities by the Egyptians and is specially blended for the Egyptian market. Coffee, because of the price, has become more of a rarity, except among the wealthy. Many of the *fellahin* are employed on larger farms, only tending their own plots in the

71

Blindfolded donkey working water-wheel at Saqqara

evening or on holidays. On the whole, work on the farms is a seven day week. Contractors arrange daily labour, for which they take a rake off, and they are paid daily rather than weekly. State insurance has now become compulsory.

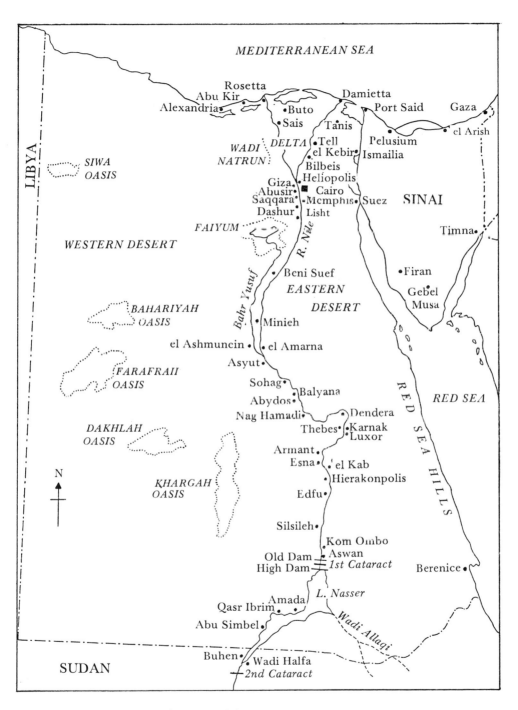

MEDITERRANEAN SEA

LIBYA

Rosetta
Abu Kir
Alexandria
Buto
Sais
Damietta
Port Said
Gaza
el Arish
Tanis
Pelusium
DELTA
Tell
el Kebir
Ismailia
WADI
NATRUN
SIWA
OASIS
Bilbeis
Heliopolis
Giza
Abusir
Cairo
Saqqara
Memphis
Suez
SINAI
Dashur
Lisht
FAIYUM
WESTERN DESERT
Timna
Beni Suef
EASTERN
Firan
Bahr Yusuf
DESERT
Gebel
Musa
BAHARIYAH
OASIS
Minieh
el Ashmunein
el Amarna
FARAFRAH
OASIS
Asyut
Sohag
Balyana
RED SEA
Abydos
Nag Hamadi
Dendera
DAKHLAH
OASIS
Thebes
Karnak
Luxor
Armant
Esna
el Kab
Hierakonpolis
KHARGAH
OASIS
Edfu
RED SEA HILLS
N
Silsileh
Kom Ombo
Old Dam
Aswan
High Dam
1st Cataract
Berenice
L. Nasser
Amada
Qasr Ibrim
Wadi Allaqi
Abu Simbel
SUDAN
Buhen
Wadi Halfa
2nd Cataract
R. Nile

Sketch map of Egypt (not to scale)

73

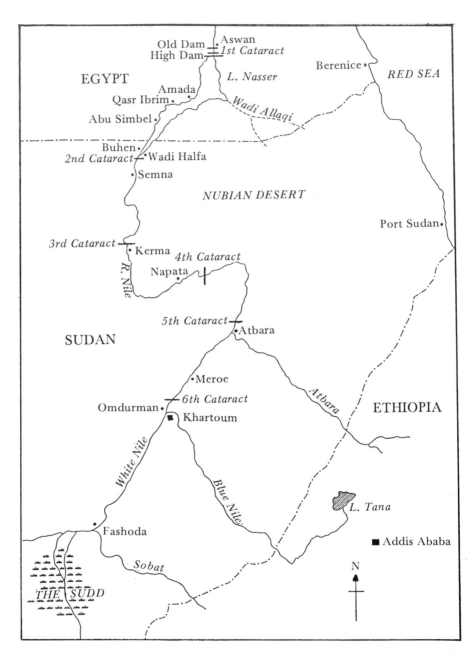

Sketch map of the Upper Nile (not to scale)

74

BIBLIOGRAPHY

B.M. = British Museum   A.U.C. = American University, Cairo
R.K.P. = Routledge & Kegan Paul

General

Seton-Williams, M.V. & Stocks, P., *Blue Guide to Egypt* (2nd ed.), A. & C. Black, 1988.
Wilson, Lt. Col. Sir A., *The Suez Canal*, O.U.P., 1933.

Land and Resources

Adams, W.Y., *Nubia, Corridor to Africa*, London, 1977.
Baines, J. & Malek, J., *Atlas of Ancient Egypt*, Phaidon Press, Oxford, 1958.
Fakry, A., *The Oases of Egypt*, Vol. I *Siwa*, Vol. II *Bahrayah and Farafra*, A.U.C., 1973/4.
James, T.G.H., *An Introduction to Ancient Egypt*, B.M., 1979.
Kees, H., *Ancient Egypt. A Cultural Topography*, London, 1961.
Rozoska, J. (ed.), *The Nile. Biology of an Ancient River*, Dr. W. Junk B.V., The Hague, 1976.
Saab, G.S., *Egyptian Agrarian Reform*, O.U.P., 1961.
Trigger, B., *Nubia Under the Pharaohs*, London, 1976.
Weeks, Kent, *Egyptology and the Social Sciences*, A.U.C., 1979.

History

Adams, C.C., *Islam and Modernism in Egypt*, O.U.P., 1933.
Ahmed, J.M., *The Intellectual Origins of Egyptian Nationalism*, O.U.P., 1960.
Aldred, C., *The Egyptians*, London, 1984.
Bevan, E., *A History of Egypt under the Ptolemaic Dynasty*, London, 1927.
Breasted, J.H., *History of Egypt*, (2nd ed.), Chicago, 1984.
Cromer, Earl of, *Abbas II*, Macmillan, 1915.
Drioton, E. & Vandier, J., *L'Egypte* (3rd ed.), Paris, 1952.
Elgood, Lt. Col. P.G., *The Ptolemies of Egypt*, Arrowsmith, 1938.
Elgood, Lt. Col. P.G., *The Later Dynasties of Egypt*, Blackwood, 1951.
Emery, W.B., *Archaic Egypt*, Penguin, 1982.
Gardiner, Sir A., *Egypt of the Pharaohs*, O.U.P., 1961.
Grant, M., *From Alexander to Cleopatra*, Weidenfeld & Nicholson, 1982.
Hill, R., *Egypt in the Sudan, 1820-1881*, O.U.P., 1959.
Holt, P.M., *Egypt and the Fertile Crescent, 1516-1922*, Longmans, 1955.
Hussaini, I.M., *The Moslem Brethren*, Khayat, Beirut, 1956.
Kitchen, K.A., *Pharaoh Triumphant (Life and Times of Ramesses II)*, Aris & Phillips, 1982.

Kitchen, K.A., *The Third Intermediate Period in Egypt*, Aris & Phillips, 1983.
Kohn, H., *History of Nationalism in the East*, Routledge, 1929.
Marsot, Afaf Lufti al-Sayyid, *Egypt in the Reign of Muhammad Ali*, C.U.P., 1984.
Muir, Sir W., *The Mamluke or Slave Dynasties of Egypt*, Smith Elder, 1896.
Bedford, D.B., *Akhenaten*, Princeton, 1984.
Seton-Williams, M.V., *Britain and the Arab States*, Luzac, 1948.
Sharaba, H.B., *Government and Politics of the Middle East in the Twentieth Century*, Van Nostrand, 1962.

Religion

Budge, E.A.W., *From Fetish to God*, O.U.P., 1930.
Cerny, J., *Ancient Egyptian Religion*, London, 1952.
Faulkner, R.O., *Ancient Egyptian Pyramid Texts*, 2 vols., O.U.P., 1969.
Faulkner, R.O., *Ancient Egyptian Coffin Texts*, 3 vols., Aris & Phillips, 1978.
Faulkner, R.O. (ed. Andrews, C.), *Book of the Dead*, B.M., 1985.
Hart, G., *A Dictionary of Egyptian Gods and Goddesses*, R.K.P., 1986.
Horning, E., *Conceptions of God in Ancient Egypt*, R.K.P., 1982.

Daily Life

Ahmar, H., *Growing up in an Egyptian Village*, R.K.P., 1966.
Bierbrier, M., *Tomb Builders of the Pharaohs*, B.M., 1982.
Blackman, W.S., *The Fellahin of Upper Egypt*, Cass, 1968.
David, Rosalie, *Pyramid Builders of Ancient Egypt*, R.K.P., 1986.
Heinzel, Fitter & Parslow, *The Birds of Britain and Europe with North Africa and the Middle East*, (3rd ed.), Collins, 1977.
Lane, E.W., *An Account of the Manners and Customs of the Modern Egyptians*, Murray, 1960.
Lewis, N., *Greeks in Ptolemaic Egypt*, Clarendon Press, 1986.
Lewis, N., *Life in Egypt under Roman Rule*, Clarendon Press, 1985.
Seton-Williams, M.V., *Egyptian Legends and Stories*, Rubicon Press, 1988.
Trigger, B.G., etc., *Ancient Egypt : a Social History*, C.U.P., 1983.

GLOSSARY

O.K. = Old Kingdom	A.E. = Ancient Egypt	Ar = Arabic
N.K. – New Kingdom	Gk – Greek	Tur = Turkish

Africanus — Sextus, Julius. A Christian traveller and writer of the Third Century A.D. who wrote a history of the world in five volumes. Probably born in Jerusalem, lived in Emmaus. May have served in the Roman army under the Emperor Septimus Severus.

Amir — Ar. (Anglicized Emir) A noble, Medieval Period.

Apopi — A serpent of gigantic size, who endangered the cosmic order by attacking Re's (sun god) boat morning and evening.

Atabak — Tur. A guardian.

Barrage — A dam across a river to control the water, with sluice gates.

Beit — Ar. House.

Bey — Tur. Turkish title.

Blemys — A camel-owning tribe from Nubia.

Byblos — Port in the Lebanon at the mouth of the Dog river, north of Beirut.

Circassians — Aristocratic, feudal tribes from the Caucasus. Muslims who recognized the suzerainty of the Sultan of Turkey. Came under Russian rule in the Eighteenth Century when many migrated to Turkey.

Clement (of Alexandria) — Titus, Flavius, Clemens (A.D. 150-215). A Christian presbyter, an important writer and teacher at the beginning of the Christian era in Alexandria. Died in exile in Asia Minor.

Crown, Red — The crown of Lower Egypt.

Crown, White — The crown of Upper Egypt.

Dahabiyah	Ar. Large sailing boat with cabins.
Deir	Ar. A monastery or convent.
East India Company	Est. 1600 as a limited company by a group of London merchants to break the monopoly of the Dutch and Portuguese trade with the East Indies. After the Indian mutiny in 1858, the company were forced to transfer their possessions in India to the English Crown.
Eusebius (of Caesarea)	A.D. 260-340. Bishop and scholar whose ecclesiastical history is the primary source for church history up to A.D. 324.
Eye of Horus	Offering made particularly to the dead. Also a talisman to ward off the evil eye.
Fellah	Ar. Plural fellahin. Egyptian peasant.
Felucca	Ar. Small sailing boat with lateen sail.
Gebal (see Jebal)	Ar. Hill or mountain.
Hapi	A.E. God of the Inundation of the Nile. Shown as a hermaphrodite figure holding plants and fish.
Heh	A.E. Anthropomorphic god, personification of infinity. Shown kneeling on a basket, holding in each hand a notched palm branch, which is the hieroglyphic sign for year.
Hittites	An Indo-European people who settled in Asia Minor in the second millennium B.C. in what was known as the Hatti land. The capital was Boğazköy, ancient Hattusas.
Horus	Horus the Elder, shown as a hawk-headed man. Horus the Younger, the son of Osiris, shown as a young boy or youth.
Id	Ar. A feast or festival.
Ideogram	Symbol expressing ideas.
Jebal (see Gebal)	Ar. Hill or mountain.
Josephus	c. A.D.37-96. Jewish priest who wrote a history of the Jews and their war against the Romans, also Contra Apion, which quotes Manetho.
Ka	A.E. term for the human double to whom all offerings were made.

78

Kadesh	City state in Central Syria on the River Orontes where Ramesses II fought the Hittite confederacy under Hattusilis. The battle was drawn, both sides claiming victory.
Khalif	Ar. Plural Khulafa. Religious ruler. Strictly successors of the Prophet Muhammad.
Kush	A.E. name for the area beyond the Second Cataract, now the Sudan, hence Kushite, a native of Kush.
Mahdi	Ar. He who is divinely guided. Muslim Messiah.
Mamluk	Ar. A slave.
Mandate	The British were given mandates to govern Palestine and Iraq by the League of Nations after the First World War.
Manetho	An Egyptian priest of the Third Century B.C. from Sebennytus, now Samannud, in the Delta, who wrote a history of Egypt.
Mariette	François, Auguste, Ferdinand (1821-1881). French. Founder of the Egyptian Department of Antiquities.
Markab	Ar. Cargo boat with sail.
Medina	Ar. A town.
Mnevis bull	Sacred bull worshipped at Heliopolis. Original capital of the Fourth nome of Upper Egypt, ancient Armant.
Mud-brick	Bricks that are left to dry in the sun as opposed to being baked in a kiln.
Mulid	Ar. A fair or festival.
Muslim Brotherhood	(Ikwan al-Muslimin). Founded in 1928 at Ismailia by Hasan al-Banna. Pro-Islamic, anti-Western movement. Now banned in Egypt.
Nabi	Ar. A prophet.
Naqada	Area in Upper Egypt famous for its Prehistoric remains. Burial place of Neith-hotep, wife of King Narmer.
Nile	Gk. Nilos.
Nubia	Area between Aswan and Wadi Halfa; name derived from nub (gold), because of the gold mines in the Wadi Alaqi.
Nun	God personifying the primeval waters, shown as a seated deity.
Ogdoad	The eight gods of Hermopolis. A.E. Khemenu. Ar. el-Ashmunein.

Origen	c. A.D. 185-254. One of the most influential theologians of the early Christian Church. Probably born in Alexandria. In A.D. 203 he became the head of the Catechetical School in Alexandria and wrote six thousand works.
Osireion	Stone temple, probably O.K., behind the Sety I temple at Abydos and usurped by him.
Osiris	God of the Underworld, identified with the dead king and with vegetation, shown as a mummified man.
Ostracon	Gk. Tile, potsherd or shell on which something is written or drawn.
Ottoman	(Osmanli). The Ottoman dynasty took its name from Osman Gazi, a Turkish leader who declared himself independent from the Seljuk Sultans after his victory at Bapdaeon in A.D. 130.
Palette	Slate for preparing eye paint. Found from the Neolithic Period onwards. In the Historic Period they were also used for describing historic events, as the Narmer palette.
Peace Conference	Held in Paris at the end of the First World War.
Petrie	Sir Mathew Flinders (1853-1942). Egyptologist who laid down the principles of excavation.
Phonogram	A written character indicating a particular spoken word.
Ptah	Creator god of Memphis, shown as a mummified human.
Pyramid Texts	Texts written inside burial chambers in pyramids from the Fifth Dynasty onwards.
Re	The Egyptian sun god usually shown as a ram-headed man.
Sais	Town in the Delta. Capital of the Twenty-sixth Dynasty, often called the Saite Dynasty.
Satrapy	Gk. A province of the Persian Empire, hence Satrap, a governor.
Scorpion macehead	A ceremonial macehead found at Hierakonpolis in a temple.
Sea Peoples	Collective name given to diverse migrating tribes who endeavoured to invade Egypt in the Twentieth Dynasty.
Sekhmet	Lion-headed goddess, wife of Ptah, guardian of the king.
Serekh	A.E. A rectangle in which is written the first of the king's five names, below which is a representation of "the palace facade".

Seth	God of Chaos shown in human form with heraldic animal head or as complete animal.
Sh'ia	Unorthodox sect of Islam. Followers of Ali, the son-in-law of the Prophet Muhammad.
Shu	God of Air, shown in human form with raised arms or with feather on head.
Sirdar	Ar. Commander in Chief.
Sokar	God of the Dead, shown as a falcon-headed man. Cult centre at Memphis.
Sublime Porte	This is a translation of the Turkish term *kapi* and referred originally to the gate of the Topkapi Palace where the Sultan heard suits and conducted governmental business. Eventually it came to mean the Ottoman Government.
Sultan	Tur. Ruler.
Tetisheri	Wife of Seqenere and the ancestress of the Eighteenth Dynasty.
Vali	Tur. Governor.
Valiyet	Tur. A province governed by a Vali.
Valley of the Kings	Burial place in rock-cut tombs of the kings of the Eighteenth to Twentieth Dynasties on the West Bank at Thebes.
Vizier	Tur. Anglicized form of Wazir. Chief minister.
Wafd	Ar. The Egyptian Nationalist party founded in November 1918 by Zagul.
Wahhabi	Ar. An Islamic community founded by Muhammad b. abd al Wahhab (1703-1787). A puritanical Sunni sect which wished to purge Islam of all later innovations. Wahhabi mosques are of a simpler design without minarets. Rosaries and the worship of saints forbidden. In 1804 the Wahhabis invaded the Hejaz and took Medina. Mecca fell two years later and Djidda soon after. By 1811 the Wahhabi Empire extended from Aleppo to the Indian Ocean and from the Persian Gulf to the Red Sea, and seriously threatened the unity of the Ottoman Empire.
Wazir	See Vizier.

INDEX

Greek Orthodox Church, 33, 62
Gulf of Aqaba, 49

Hajj, 67
Hathor, 12
Hatshepsut, 20, 27
Hejaz, 35, 38, 42
Heliopolis, 12, 28, 58, 59
Hellenistic, 20, 32
Heraclius, Emperor, 34
Hermopolis, 58
Herodotus, 24
Hierakonpolis, 22
Hieroglyphs, 6, 13, 14, 17, 18, 39
High Dam, 2, 13, 54, 56
Hittites, 27, 29, 30
Horus, 16, 21, 23, 59, 61
Horus Aha, 23
Horus, Battle of, 21
Horus Name, 16, 25
Hussain, Kamil, Sultan, 50
Hyksos, 11, 26

Ibn Talun Mosque, 34
Ibrahim Pasha, 42
Id al-Fatr, 63
Ikshids, 35
Imam of Yemen, 54
Imhotep, 24, 60
Incubator, 71
India, 1, 8, 39, 65
Inundation, 2, 4, 6, 20, 24, 57, 58
Irrigation, 4, 7, 22, 45, 51, 53
Islam, 34, 37, 38, 62, 63, 68
Ismail Pasha, 43, 44, 50
Ismail, 7th Imam, 35
Israel, 30, 53, 54
Issus, 32
Istanbul, 38, 39, 42
Italian-Abyssinian War, 52
Itj-Towy (Lisht), 25

Jahwar, 35
Jerusalem, 35, 36
Jews, 53, 64
Jordan, 56
Josephus, 14

Ka (Karim), 16, 70
Kadesh, 29
Kaima, 4
Kemet, 2
Kephre, 11
Khafre, 24
Khalif, 35-38
Khalifate, 34, 35
Khartoum, 46, 47

Khasekhemwy, 23
Khedives, 40
Khnum 12, 58
Khufu, 24
King Lists, 14, 22
Kitchener, Lord, 47, 49, 50
Kom Ombo, 11
Konia, 42
Kush, 31

Lake Nasser (Sudd el-Ali), 3, 13, 57
Language, 17, 18
Law, 65, 68
Lebanon, 9, 25, 27
Libyans, 25, 30, 31
Lloyd, Lord, 52
Louis, Saint, 37
Lower Egypt, 1, 4, 11, 12, 16, 17, 21, 58, 60
Luxor, 12

Ma'at, 60
Mahdi, 46, 47
Mahdist Revolt, 45
Malakef, 66
Mamluk, 37-39
Mamluk Beys, 40
Manetho, 14, 26
Mansura, 37
Mariette, Auguste, 67
Marriage, 70
Marseilles, 40
Martyr's Calendar, 62
Mastaba, 67
Mawalid, 64
McMahon, Sir Henry, 50
Mecca, 34, 37, 47, 63, 67
Mediterranean, 1, 13, 40
Medjay, 65
Memphis, 1, 11, 12, 17, 21, 31, 60, 61
Menes, 14, 21, 23
Mentu-Hotep, 25
Merneptah, 30
Meroe, 4, 30
Middle East, 1, 6, 12, 37
Middle Kingdom, 12, 14, 25
Milner, Lord, 51
Misr (Egypt), 1
Mnevis Bull, 12
Monasticism, 62
Mongols, 37
Monophistic Church, 62
Morea, 42
Mubarak, President, 56
Muhammad (Prophet), 35, 63, 64
Muhammad Ali, 40, 42, 43, 45
Muhammad Bey el-Alfi, 40